Your Life in My Hands

Hear It Now! Hear It Now! Hear It Now!

Pamela Rose

WestBow Press®
A DIVISION OF THOMAS NELSON
& ZONDERVAN

Copyright © 2017 Pamela Rose.

All rights reserved. No part of this book may be used or reproduced by any means, graphic, electronic, or mechanical, including photocopying, recording, taping or by any information storage retrieval system without the written permission of the author except in the case of brief quotations embodied in critical articles and reviews.

Scripture taken from the New King James Version®. Copyright © 1982 by Thomas Nelson. Used by permission. All rights reserved.

This book is a work of non-fiction. Unless otherwise noted, the author and the publisher make no explicit guarantees as to the accuracy of the information contained in this book and in some cases, names of people and places have been altered to protect their privacy.

WestBow Press books may be ordered through booksellers or by contacting:

WestBow Press
A Division of Thomas Nelson & Zondervan
1663 Liberty Drive
Bloomington, IN 47403
www.westbowpress.com
1 (866) 928-1240

Because of the dynamic nature of the Internet, any web addresses or links contained in this book may have changed since publication and may no longer be valid. The views expressed in this work are solely those of the author and do not necessarily reflect the views of the publisher, and the publisher hereby disclaims any responsibility for them.

Cover Artwork: Anabel Heredia Art & Design
Cover Photography: Alexis Wiener

ISBN: 978-1-9736-1782-2 (sc)
ISBN: 978-1-9736-1781-5 (hc)
ISBN: 978-1-9736-1783-9 (e)

Library of Congress Control Number: 2018901252

Print information available on the last page.

WestBow Press rev. date: 2/8/2018

To my family and those I do and don't know, whoever I may be to you, whether a mum, daughter, sister, aunty, great-aunty, cousin, friend, or stranger, this book is true, inspired, and penned for you. May you hear its voice as it speaks to your heart, just as it did to mine and as I lived its every page! Some, of course, were more colorful than others were, but all are part of my journey's story!

The lengths to which God, our Father and Creator, pursued me serves to demonstrate His patience, forbearance, and, most of all, His infinite love for us, His children. If only we could learn not to fight against Him so much but instead accept His gift of grace and forgiveness in gratitude and love, then our personal journey may be that much lighter. For I know that I know that I know. Do you?

Contents

Acknowledgments xi
Introduction xiii
Part 1   The Early Years 1
Part 2   The Teens 9
Part 3   The Battleground 16
Part 4   New Life 22
Part 5   Crunch Time! 30
Chapter 1   Thursday, Day 1 34
Chapter 2   Friday, Day 2 37
Chapter 3   Saturday, Day 3 41
Chapter 4   Sunday, Day 4 48
Chapter 5   Monday, Day 5 54
Chapter 6   Tuesday, Day 6 57
Chapter 7   Why So Long? 61
Chapter 8   So What Next? 65
Chapter 9   Terra Firma 70
Chapter 10   Change 74
Chapter 11   Chayil! 81
Chapter 12   Let's Begin Again 90
Epilogue 95

Hear it Now! Hear it Now! Hear it Now!

God is our life,
the breath of our soul,
the secret place in you and me.
God is!

God is our hope,
the rescue of the heart
when love kidnapped is taken.
God forever is!

God is the way,
the path to our home,
eternally lit for mankind to see.
God is eternal!

So, when senses distract,
think but do not conclude,
for we think wrong.

We think knowledge,
eager to teach and dictate,
erroneous organic matter voicing!

God knows …
God thinks …
God is
in the very matter of that organ,
whispering,
"Listen, child of mine, child of promise.
Listen to words that feed and nourish
my word, my heart, and my love.
My eternity in you delivered

In my Son Jesus Christ.
Hear it now!
Hear it now!
Hear it now!"

Pamela Rose
Southlake, Texas

Acknowledgments

What does an acknowledgment look life when God's provision, whether material or spiritual, has filled your life to overflowing? So many people have crossed my intricately woven path. I suppose I am not sure, and so I thank those close and afar who have shared joys and sorrows, love and despair, and life and death together with me thus far. Thank you for being there!

I have put this book together because God broke into my reverie, stirred my dormant being, and said, "Rise." This is the result, Pamela Rose. My being saved doesn't make any sense unless you see my former life in all its abysmal disarray.

And to God, my Creator, my heavenly Father, I acknowledge and thank you for pursuing me into acknowledgment.

So there you go! This is what it looks like, Pamela Rose. And to Him, I say, "Thank you."

Introduction

Just one word first! I need to set the scene so you can understand this book. It has a beginning and a middle but does not have an end. Well, not just yet! It's been written for you.

"But who is you?" I hear you think.

Well, it is my family, friends, acquaintances, and even those I have never met. But for those who do know me, they will understand this story is authentic me.

You will discover as and if you read on that I found myself in America at the end of 2006. How and why has only been made known to me over the past ten years. Yes, it is 2017, and this book is only now being given life. Why? It was conceived when I was born again, and its message had to be written in the hours, days, weeks, months, and years that followed my five-day retreat on a remote Southern Texas ranch. I had to experience God's hand upon me before I could fully experience His will because it's not about me, my husband, or my son. No, it's all about God through Jesus Christ in the message of His cross. This is my why and His because.

Everything you will read happened. It always had divine purpose, and I am to share it with you. There are no frills. It has a voice, it speaks aloud, and I am the pen for that voice.

And so it is with unconditional love that I now release to you the beginning, namely *Your Life in My Hands* and the middle-named "Hear It Now! Hear It Now! Hear It Now." Like I said, there is no end yet, for that is a work in progress.

I know the thaw is on its way, and some hardened hearts among you may start to melt. You too can flow in His divine river of love as it spills over into your life's unique currents and into your why and His because. Receive it today while time still ticks, for the clock will expire and, with it, our precious lives.

"Hear it now," each bird declared.
"Hear it now," the shrill note pierced.
"Hear it now," time demanded.

Now is the time to hear His voice alighting in your heart.
Now is the time to hear His heart penetrating your soul.
Now is the time to hear His soul becoming one with you.
Now is the time to hear you embrace His goodness.
Now is the time to hear His goodness explain why.
"Because I love you."

Part 1

The Early Years

We all start life the same way. We are born and take our first breath. There is no disputing the fact. It is a universal truth. Now how we are delivered into this world and where, are quite different matters. Our differences begin immediately and continue until that very last breath is drawn and we extinguish. In between the first and the last is a lifetime of diversity, and therein lies the mystery. Who are you? Who am I? Why am I here?

To understand the relevance and magnitude of this testimony, you must first understand my diversity in all its futility and my rescue in all its glory. The words "I was lost but now am found" had been but Sunday morning words chanted intermittently for fifty-three years, but now my raison d'être exists. My why and because were told.

Please join me on a global tour where Hollywood scripts could find inspiration and where hearts draw solace, for the choice is quite simply yours with no coercion, browbeating, Bible bashing, or guilt trips. It's just an invitation to step into our Creator's presence and see His plans unfold His way. You will be able to see His will in one person's life, and that person is me.

Many will be mumbling that they don't care, but if you are one of those, then I challenge you to read this story and absorb its truths, reflect, and then pose the question "Who cares?" thereafter. If you remain unmoved, then I offer no apologies, for my task is but to plant. Someone else will water this seed, and *only one* can cause you to grow. And you must discover Him personally. No one can do that for you.

As I was saying, we are all born. Agreed? Good. We can now move forward harmoniously. I was born in a small hospital in Melrose, Massachusetts. I recall nothing of the event, but I was the third daughter, the youngest sibling. As an American by birth and with parents of mixed nationalities—one Yank and one English rose, a GI bride to be precise—my trek began. I use the term *trek* for it often seemed like I was traipsing back and forth across the Atlantic, while my parents attempted to satisfy revolving pangs of homesickness, none of which ever seemed to be satiated.

"Never marry a cow out of your pasture," my mother would say from time to time throughout my life when yet another trek proved fruitless.

I didn't get her drift at the time, but I do now. A common English language was shared between my parents, but that was where the similarities ended. My parents' respective families were at opposite ends of the spectrum. My father was a Bostonian of Irish descent, and he was Catholic. My mother, a fair English rose, had a good, solid ancestry and a Protestant background. The US family was extensive, and hard working. And some among them were prone to drinking excessively. Have you ever heard of a teetotalist Irishman? (No offense is intended, of course. I speak in generalities.)

While the British contingent was small and not partial to drinking to excess, although the odd "G&T" never went amiss, they were moneymakers. One of them today boasts millions, is a tax exile into the bargain, and, dare I suggest, unhappy. It's life's irony at its best, but that is quite a separate tale of woe. The devastation that can be wrought in the pursuit of money is unsettling and, yes, predictable. It certainly has served to illustrate that a person cannot serve two masters.

So, how does an English Protestant marry an American Catholic? Quite simply, she doesn't. My mother had to undergo the rigors of the catechism in order to qualify for the exclusive club before membership was granted. This she duly did for her debonair, American Air Force officer who swept her off her feet in the closing days of World War II in Bristol, England.

The year was 1944. The proposed union was, of course, met with immediate disapproval from a disappointed British father who was mindful that he would be losing his fair English rose to distant shores. Still, the union was happily met with warm approval from a supportive mother and sister.

Love had brought them together, and love bound them through perilous matrimonial territories for fifty-four years until my dear father was called home. Although my knowledge of God was commensurate with the teaching of the Catholic church—and for that I leave the mind to determine individually—at the time of his passing, I knew that he knew God existed. His Catholic dogma was not a legacy to embrace, but his insistence every night that as a child I should say my prayers was tantamount to a holy witness and a seed unwittingly sewn. For that I am deeply grateful.

However, I was not so grateful for the hypocrisy that Catholicism engendered for me otherwise until March 4, 2007. This is my personal experience and opinion, and no offense is intended to any reader. It merely reflects my view and experiences only. I have no wish to defame anyone or anybody by my life story. It is my truth, and I bear the scars.

I spent the first four years of my life in Wakefield, Massachusetts, with two older sisters. Sadly, the eldest has now returned to her maker, and in heaven she peacefully reclines. My recollection of Wakefield is scant, and other than learning to ice-skate on double blades in the trusting arms of my father on the local lake, memories are few. My father had been blessed to be a fine sportsman, even to the point of having a tryout for a prominent Boston ice hockey team. I am told that one of his nephews did make the team, but I never really got to know the American contingent of the family.

Ice hockey was but one of my father's sporting passions, and the other was golf. Had the clutch of World War II not made its grab, his life might have taken quite a different circuit—and advisedly, I am told—in the field of golf. But alas, pesky wars do have a habit of invading people's lives and at the most inconvenient times.

My father's work at Pan American (Pan Am) Airways made way for our first escapade across the world and this time to Keflavik, Iceland. Yes, I was to leave the comfort of suburban US living to experience life and my first school in a strangely foreign land and culture. We were to spend two and a half years in an almost barren landscape. Not a tree or flower was to be seen. It was just rack upon rack of dried, pungent fish lining the roads and well-padded sheep treading the craggy escarpments that formed the immediate terrain. It was stark and dark. It was, however, my home.

We lived in a small yet comfortable house, and our neighbors were British. Thank heavens for small mercies! It was a definite comfort for my mother, who always pined for her home shores. My first memorable memory, if you can say that, was the arrival home one evening of my father with two husky puppies in the back of the Land Rover. They were named Krona and Ora, and they became my best friends.

I discovered early that my weekly excursion with my mother into Keflavik to purchase the dreaded diet of fresh fish, namely halibut and esau, always excluded my beloved friends. I was told that they would be shot on sight if seen in the car, and whether this was true, to this day I know not. What I do know is that it raised in me an unhealthy fear and a first step into the world of worry. Oh, how subtle are the trappings of deception as they are set in an unsuspecting soul's life!

The years in Iceland were harsh climatically, but they afforded a child the happy memories of being snowbound in one's own home, coupled with carefree abandonment amid the snow's gleaming beauty. I loved the snow, as did my dogs.

Christmas was a special time in this Northern Hemisphere, and Santa Claus always seemed closer on the northern horizons as changing lights danced across crimson-colored skies, the aurora borealis, God's indescribable wonder to behold, and now a colorful memory.

Iceland was my home for over two years until it was time to up sticks again and embark on the next trek. This time, it would be fifteen hundred miles east to my mother's homeland and my first encounter with England, minus one of my friends, Ora, who had mysteriously disappeared. Krona became a part of the family for many years, and he was duly shipped to England. It involved six months of quarantine, but he was without doubt a family member, fully subscribed and loved. Ora became but a childhood memory.

Bristol was our home and the birthplace of my mother, but it was never my father's home. His heart belonged to America, and there it remained. I had my seventh birthday in England, and I was promptly sent to a local Catholic girl's school, accompanied by my two elder sisters.

For the eldest, the whole experience was unacceptable, and she deeply resented being in the United Kingdom. She was fifteen years old when she first set foot on British soil, and fitting into the education system was for her a no-go area. America was her home, and she was not going to cooperate.

Unfortunately, my childhood saw the birth of an ever-widening rift between my mother and this very American sister. Wounds were inflicted, and deep resentments were set in motion. Mum was English, so surely it must have been her fault for dragging the family across the seas. Why go to England after Iceland? Why not return to the United States, her home? It was more change, more adjustment, and more friends to make. It was all too much for her, and the road of rebellion was chosen. What she did not know was the true reason for leaving icy Iceland. Later life would shed its secret, but for young children and adolescent teenagers, caring parents thought best to shield the truth.

Now my first home in England was not just a home. It was a pub called the Highbury Vaults, and for the next five years, it provided all our needs. The most unusual thing about our tenancy, for breweries then owned the pubs, namely "Georges" at the time, was the fact that my father was the first American to ever be granted a British publican's license. It was considered newsworthy because of its scarcity. However, in our case, the only problem with living in a pub is if your father's penchant is for alcohol and its draw would be tested inordinately. It's then tantamount to suicide. Put a child in a sweet shop, and what will he or she do?

I have clearer memories of life moving forward and the Highbury Vaults, which is still there today, provided me with a measure of solace but also embarrassment. The English, being very class conscious, rather looked down on tradespeople, and I distinctly recall feeling uneasy at having to admit to school friends that my mother worked, not least in a pub.

We did have a cleaning lady which helped a little in my mind, but my introduction to classifying people by address, profession, and accent began. I was put onto the treadmill of class distinction, even discrimination, with all its vulgarity, and there I was left to scramble. One peculiarity of the British is that money cannot buy class under any circumstances. It's an elitist club in every sense. Only the right school, family background, and Queen's English permits entry. I even had the misfortune of recently dining in London and being questioned about my unfortunate surname at that time, namely Sullivan.

"Oh, you must be from Irish stock," was the deadly poison sarcastically ejaculated from the mouth of a less than agreeable lady.

My response was equally perilous as I too had inherited the alcohol addiction and, with it, a blistering, treacherous tongue. I had enjoyed a class or two of vino that evening, and she reaped its venom.

In the Highbury Vaults, alcohol and coal fires surrounded me. Strangers downstairs were consuming my parents' time, and many mice entered into the equation. Cats were then introduced to combat these unwelcome houseguests. Admittedly they served to lessen the overpopulation of the four-legged creatures that scurried in our cellars and silently under floorboards throughout, but they also gave birth to allergies. Puffy red eyes, runny nose, and sneezing became a daily occurrence, but went by undetected.

Just part of life, was my thinking.

My friend Krona was always beside me, adding to this growing problem with animals, but it just didn't seem to raise alarm bells for anyone. It was only in later years when I was eleven that the concept I might have an allergy was diagnosed. Removing the cat was easy. But the dog? Never! I would live with the sneezing and itchy eyes. Krona was my most loyal Icelandic friend.

My pub years saw the disappearance of my father back to his homeland from time to time, and I remember gazing out of my bedroom window in the evenings, half-expecting to see him walking down the road, but that was just childish thinking at the time. Yes, he did return, but his heart remained in Boston.

Living in a pub was not altogether wise when the problem was alcohol, but it did provide much needed income. In the event, another move was necessary. This time it was just four miles down the road to a very large, eleven-bedroom home on the Downs in Bristol, a parks area that the Merchant Venturers donated to each citizen of Bristol over a century before. It was enormous and even had those wonderful bells audible and visible in the breakfast room when being pressed from somewhere in the house above.

Upstairs/downstairs, for sure. I was nicknamed the "runner" during those years, as it was my task to run the height, length, and breadth of the house every time I was requisitioned for some small task, invariably by my mother. This label unfortunately stuck. Don't you just hate pet names?

Sightings of my father once again became infrequent for a whole host of reasons, and I vividly recall the miserable task as runner to dash to the local (the pub) and tell him dinner was ready, but to no avail. He would invariably return home hours later, slightly worse for wear and a cold dinner alone in the oven, while my discouraged mother hovered.

I dreaded those evenings, and I think I left my father behind somewhere in my childhood. His love affair with alcohol gained momentum, took precedence over all else, including work, and contributed to yet more fear mongering for me. Insecurity took up residence within my unknowing soul, and doubt and fear married. Unhealthy allegiances were formed and remained fiercely held until release was possible in the years ahead.

The change of house had brought with it a change of school. I had taken a Common Entrance Exam, usual in 1960s England, and won a place at yet another Catholic school, this time La Retraite High School for Girls, again in Bristol. It was more nuns and more unhealthy fear communicated, yet some wonderful years of sports. I played on the teams for multiple-school sports, including field hockey, netball, and tennis. I lived for my sports and spent many hours lost in its competitive lure. I was not a star, but good enough to be counted.

The Southwest Tennis Circuit was my claim to fame, and smatterings of county tennis were played. Being the school's singles tennis champion was a memory worth holding, while many doubles titles were also added to my confidence belt. Wimbledon became my passion early in life, and I was fortunate enough to be part of the center court crowd on many occasions. At least I could sit there and dream.

Part 2

The Teens

At thirteen years old, the family was on the move again, this time back to the US, back home. Or was England home? I never really knew where I fitted in, but as a child, you duly obeyed and went where you were told. I had frequently been taught that 'children should be seen and not heard.' For me, it was the cause of much juvenile, mental paralysis. It was a label worn by many an English child, suppressive in its purpose and oppressive in its effects. We are unceremoniously sewn into fear, and we drown in its pull as we are sucked along life's diverse channels, never knowing when the levels are going to rise above one's survival instincts.

My elder sister, whom you will recall, never accepted the move to England. She did not form part of this next trek back to my father's homeland. She remained in England. Lost in love to a local lad, she became single-minded in perspective. She loved him, and that was the end of story. Or was it just the beginning of diversity for her and our family? Yes, indeed it was, but again this is the subject of another story.

For forty-eight years they were married until her death in 2015. How strong that bond of love can be, no matter what it appears like to those looking from without in. It is a bizarre line drawn when one cannot live with a person but simultaneously cannot live without that individual, an irony that many discover and endure on this side of eternity.

The move back to America was a *fait accompli*, and my sister, not disposed to returning now as love had captured her heart, left an anxious mother in the unenviable position of having to make the right decision for her. My father had once again disappeared from the scene to set up home for us in the US, while Mother closed camps in England.

My mother always seemed to be left holding the reins and was the wicked taskmaster from my sister's perspective. She was not, of course. She was just a good mother trying to hold together an alcohol-affected marriage and the fringes of teenage selfishness. I applaud her now and respect her unfailing bravery throughout. She adhered to those marriage vows for richer or poorer and in sickness and in health, but she bore the brunt. Thankfully, the deep love for her American officer bade her stay, and the sanctity of marriage allowed her to survive. And we, as children, were given the privilege of retaining two parents and a home. I wonder whether the same can be said of marriage today?

Our return to America in 1966 was a time of much upheaval and enormous sadness. Not only did I have to leave my home, my school friends, and my beloved school sports, my sister was going to remain in Bristol. It became agony for me knowing she was not going to be in my life anymore, and I did not understand. I sobbed endless nights into my pillow, but never did I divulge my sorrow. I just skipped along as children do (seen and not heard) and buried sadness deep into my being for later exhumation.

It was another school. And guess what? Yes, it was another Catholic school. This time, it was the Academy of Our Lady of Nazareth for Girls in Wakefield, Massachusetts, which has now closed its doors. Yes, it was more nuns, more dogma, and more change. Although my years said eighth grade, my school records spoke otherwise, and I was placed in high school at the tender age of thirteen years, the youngest pupil in the school.

Fitting in was not easy, and had it not been for my wonderful neighbor friend, Lisa, I do not think I would have survived the year. She was my security. We were of the same age, and she was a wonderful girl, one of twelve children born into a Bostonian

Catholic family that lived next door. She did not judge me or the obvious discrepancy in our respective family's income brackets. She was my friend, and I longed to finish school each day just so I could go to their palatial home and be included. She was an eighth grader at the local high school where my next-eldest sister also attended.

Now my move to America was not all bad for my other lifetime friend, Krona, was duly shipped over with us. My mother sailed on the *SS United States* with him duly in stow. Yes, it was another quarantine period to be endured, but he was a family member.

My mother's arrival into New York's dock was apparently reminiscent of her earlier arrival as a GI bride back in 1946 aboard the *Queen Mary*. Something special about that 1946 moment was the fact that it was recorded for prosperity sake. TV footage showed a young newlywed English girl running madly down the gangplank into the arms of her beau as she was being swept off her feet and spun midair. The scene evoked the attention of the press as well as TV, and the newspaper cutting remains in our family box.

Now what is even more intriguing about this event was the fact that, forty-five years on from that day, my two parents sat at home watching a wartime documentary on GI brides in Bristol, England. I also happened to be sitting with them that evening. Now what footage do you suppose came up on the TV? Yes, the two of them taken in 1946!

For me, it was a moment of adulation that those were my parents on the television, along with love that they were still enjoined. They were visibly moved by the realization and recollection of a moment in time captured and now relived forty-five years on in their living room. Oh, where is that TV footage? Can anyone out there help me? I am sure my mother would enjoy reliving those moments again.

But twelve months after settling into another set of surroundings and circumstances, another move further muddied life. Yes, we were going back to England again. The move back to Wakefield, Massachusetts, had been a disaster from start to finish, and my dear father's attempts to discard the bottle, unsuccessful. A mother with two children in the US with insufficient income and one daughter in the UK was a heavy burden for any mother. At least if she returned to the UK, it was her pasture. Her brother lived there, and she could eke out an income more easily and be with her daughter.

My mother once again was the stalwart, and she returned first with her two girls to set up home again. Father remained in the US in an effort to regain dignity and formulate composure. Leaving his six brothers and sisters for the umpteenth time, plus countless nephews and nieces, could not have been easy, but he was still married and loved his English rose despite all. He must follow, and this he did.

My beloved Krona was never seen again. I was told he was given to friends who owned a large ranch and wanted to keep him. I believed their lie for ages until reality struck. He had obviously been put down, and to this day, I am saddened. Maybe I will see him again one day in doggie heaven.

Bristol was to be our home once again, and a return to my former school, my comfort. I remained there until my sixth form years were over, but not without pain. At the ripe old age of eighteen years and my final year at school, I entered into enemy territory and tasted the bitterness of forbidden love. I walked headlong into quicksand and slowly sank mercilessly into the mire. I was eighteen years old; he was thirty-two, almost old enough to be my father. He cast his line, and I took the bait. I seized the well-dressed businessman, the flashy car, and apparent wealth.

In hindsight, I was grasping at any form of male security I could find, perhaps a father figure, but at the time, it was a buzz, and so began my demise, even before my birth. I was a schoolgirl dressed in compulsory uniform and as innocent as a rose bears thorns. I became yet another of his prey, but this time with a difference. He too was pricked, and we thought we loved one another. The spell had been cast, and I was totally captivated. Illicit love it was, but there appeared to be no escape. We started to run together, and the debris left behind, widely strewn.

With school exams taken and passed and graduation complete, it was time to leave Bristol to attend college in Southern England. Two terms at a Catholic college in Southampton came to an abrupt end with mutually pining hearts and my ambition to become a French teacher shelved permanently. I was to forego all in the name of love. Blinded, I quickly enrolled in a two-year bilingual secretary's course in a local technical college to be closer to him, and my mock role was further established.

I had joined the broad and wide road said to lead to destruction, and I attired myself in folly's entourage of disguises. I justified my decision to leave Southampton without even considering my faithful mother's perspective. I think I could have written a handbook on how to be a selfish madame with little or no effort because "all about me" became my tour de force. I was to become yet another victim of deception, but my eyes only saw the bright, chintzy lights of affluent poverty.

Staying at home was no longer a possibility for me, and an anxious mother wisely disciplining an errant daughter became just words. I would not—could not—listen. I was in love! By this time, my sister had married her young merchant seaman. As I said, thoughts of my mother's welfare never crossed my mind for selfishness was my robe and self-destruction my elective. My heart would not permit me to listen to wisdom in abundance from many sources, and the curse of the bottle became my companion. I too had inherited a predisposition to alcohol, wholly unsuited to my particular personality, which subsequently proved to be my downfall through the ensuing years. There's shameless living and solace in a bottle! What more lethal recipe could be concocted, but later life revealed my truth. I was being held in His safe hold until I could see, and this created …

Someone Like Me!

I was afraid.
I was afraid to dare
to think you could love
someone like me,
someone like me
whose heart has seen the darker side
of love that stole my youth,
my joy,
my hope!

I am broken
I am broken to recall
all that I squandered over
and over again and again,
blinded by obsession,
betrayed by love,
and battered by all that love was never meant to be!

I will see
I will see His love
showing me how to live again
with no shame or pain,
for all is well for those who dare to trust His love
once for all
eternally given, to someone like me!

***

It all makes sense now, but during those halcyon days of self first and the "who cares" attitude firmly in place, I squandered countless years on frivolity and folly. I suspect it is a place where many of us have parked indifference and laissez-faire attitudes unwittingly or even unknowingly. God was distant, and the human conscience was but an irritant to be scratched and temporarily satisfied until the next twinge at least.

My strict Catholic upbringing did not provide the foundation of faith needed to walk in truth, and I too had swallowed the lie. I had been deceived and did not have a clue who the person of Jesus Christ was. All I knew was obligatory church and holy days of obligation, no meat on Fridays, Latin masses, and veiled heads. I had never been taught the Bible, merely rote Sunday services chanted by disinterested, lifeless priests. (No disrespect is intended. I'm just telling you how it was for me then.)

In Catholicism, I learned how hypocrisy operated, at least from my personal perspective. Sin all week long, do as you wish, and then make your confession on Saturday and attend mass on Sunday, of course! What could be easier and more convenient than that?

At many a Christmas midnight mass, I recall the whiff of alcoholic breaths singing in unison and lacing the atmosphere. Such were the many there to satisfy doctrinal dogma. For me, the Catholic conscience was an almighty battleground from whence I crawled some thirty-five years later, but not without serious wounds. Coming into God's light was on the horizon, but for now, it was an unknown quantity. For now, it was all about number one. Moi!

Part 3

The Battleground

Stepping from innocence into temptation and beyond set the stage for life's diversity to further intensify, and the glare of heaven was firmly hidden from my view. I saw only the world and all that it did and did not have to offer. I scurried from pit to pit, never stopping to consider the open prison in which I was being held.

The chapter of forbidden love was long and excruciatingly painful. It bore untold anguish and buried me alive. I could not see life, only slow seduction into money's masterful hold. And all the while, real life was passing me by. How deep is my grave of regret! My attempts to sever the stranglehold of love led me back to the US, Houston this time, but it was a fruitless exercise. I was pursued, and my heart was torn further apart.

I remained for two years working at the corporate headquarters of an oil giant, laying the foundation of a long friendship that eventually would lead me back to the US some thirty years later. God's plan was silently unfolding.

Lifestyle in Houston was fast moving and wild. Happy hours galore and a bounty of men were entering my web. It was the mid-1970s, and this was boomtown in Texas. One in particular showed me the rich and famous of Houston, Bimini, Cat Cay, the Bahamas, Acapulco, Aspen, and Vail, and I continued to squander my life in vain pursuit of nothingness. Alcohol remained my constant companion, and it led me into many treacherous encounters. Private jet travel mixed with luxury yachts and the requisite Mercedes sports car. I merely supplemented my English forbidden love for an American version, except this time our ages were slightly more respectable.

Lasting friendships were forged from this US foray, as were memory lanes. It was a time of gross trivial pursuit and gay abandon. Youth was on my side, but a heavy heart became my millstone. My past soul ties would not go away, and the promise of a home and empty gifts rendered me putty in ever-selfish hands. I left the oil-rich land and headed home. What I had achieved in the fleeting sojourn was uncertain, but later years would reveal its purpose.

My experience album was indeed expanding, but so too was the scar tissue. Indelible blots and stepping-stones were leading deeper into the abyss, and I didn't once notice. Blindfolded by selfish love, I returned.

The 1980s brought with it unspeakable selfishness, only matched by the havoc it wrought. Innocent lives were wounded by flagrant and flippant disregard for all that is held sacred in life. I was a smash-and-grab artiste extraordinaire, skipping and squandering precious years in exchange for self-fulfillment in whatever form that would take.

Qualified as a bilingual secretary in French and Spanish, I put some of it to good use in a job that was initially based in Bristol and later in London. Working at main board level for an international corporation added to the mayhem. Now I was to ride on the back of another's success. I did not know who I was. I was lost and like a raft in a raging ocean. I was being tossed back and forth, never finding the destination.

During the London years, envy took hold silently, seductively and surely. I grew disgruntled with being just a secretary and earning a pittance. I enjoyed the benefits of chauffeur-driven cars and even corporate jet travel when accompanying my boss to overseas board meetings, but this was not enough. I became arrogant and compounded it by setting an impossible challenge. I wanted to complete a law degree and then become a solicitor while working full time in London.

Because I wanted it all, I put myself through untold misery to achieve the goal. A four-year course at night school was embarked upon and successfully completed. I had attempted and achieved the deemed impossible. The forbidden lover finally became redundant, and my captive heart, hardened beyond recognition, was now able to cope alone, or so I thought. My high-flyer job took precedence, and levels of indulgent behavior intensified, so much so that I actively disliked myself.

The conscience thankfully would kick in every so often, reminding me of what was right and wrong, but more importantly, that intangible yet real truth what I ought to be doing prodded. Deep down, I knew that my life was positively empty despite being prima facie, full. Overflowing with sickening depravity might have been an apt description, and possibly my self-admonishment today may be a trifle harsh but needed. Those I offended and affected must be the judge, but condemnation is no longer my cloak. Thank you, Jesus. Thank you.

The commute from London to Bristol to attend evening classes was gruesome, and in the fourth and final year, it took its toll. I believe I suffered a nervous breakdown requiring some six weeks away from work. During this break, I flew to Barcelona with my faithful mother to board a classy cruise liner for a two-week Mediterranean cruise. On this trip, I met and laid the foundation of a strong friendship with a South African family, with whom I would remain close friends. The relevance of this meeting will become clear presently. Surely God was always ahead of me in His plans thankfully.

Now it was back to the law! The four years studying for my law degree while retaining a full-time, demanding job in London was smattered with hope in the shape of a dear and loyal co-student who dutifully gathered all notes should I miss a class. Many a night would I arrive late from traffic problems or returning from a day's excursion overseas, whether to Spain, Paris, or Zurich. I even recall a couple occasions when the company jet was returning executives to Bristol and I would hitchhike a ride back. My wonderful family was always there to support me and whisk me across Bristol to jurisprudence, land law, and criminal law in order to attend requisite classes.

The four-year feat was achieved, and I was awarded my Bachelor of Law degree in 1987, presented to me by Sir Patrick Mayhew, then Attorney General. It was an honor, and my precious and wise confidante mother duly attended the graduation ceremony.

But the sting in the tail in this story was the fact that, if I wanted to now become a solicitor (lawyer in US speak), I would have to resign from my glamorous London job. I was a creature possessed and driven.

Thankfully I was made redundant and enrolled in the mandatory, one-year, full-time Law Society finals course again in Bristol. This was an immensely intense and lonely nine months of unending study, which I, along with many other aspiring lawyers, survived, and successfully completed. I passed the exams. Was I now a solicitor? No! Another two years training lay ahead of me, this time at a prestigious law firm where I completed my Articles. I hated every minute of it. It was life's irony at its best!

I endured the two years. At its end, was admitted to the Bar in 1990, and my name was entered on the Roll. I had achieved the impossible. Early on in my studies, I recall one of the board directors, an ex-Etonian no less, with an accent to match, telling me I couldn't possibly achieve the task I had set before me. His condescension was partly responsible for the insatiable drive I had embraced, wanting to prove him wrong.

My wildness had not decreased, and alcohol remained my companion. This time it took me into waters I had not yet chartered, but ironically put me in an invisible boat with a rudder, map, compass, and destination.

God's plans are so exacting when executed. He's always in control, no matter the texture of your life's fabric, and now is His time. Heed it!

Now!

Marvelous is the victory to be won
when first we learn to trust in Him,
God our Father, friend, and strength.
We learn each lesson in the mistake
and difficulty but evidence of His guidance,
for if we overcome, victory is ours.
So learn each lesson quickly.
Overcome weakness, wrong
and not that done to you!

Standards must be high, for His highest.
As your life surges to the crest of the wave,
see Him walking alongside, reassuring
"Be of good cheer. It is I. Do not be afraid."
Oh, the comfort, the promise here given!
Depend and lean on Him, on His powers alone,
for you have none without Him, none!
His purpose is your destination.
His Love, your protection.

Can you remain calm in the turmoil
unperplexed as waves dash against your life?
His end for you, for me, is the Way.
He walks on our waves towards us,
always encouraging when no land is in view.
No success to savor, no goal to glorify.
He walks with you, so learn fast!
Keep Him in sight, that promise to behold.
God teaches. God constrains. God trains.
For now is the moment. Now!

No future wish list or glamorous goal, to yearn,
    but training, and preparing daily His design
        for you, for me, for all to see
        that minute by minute, hour to hour,
     He manages all chaos alongside, our now.
   All eyes must be on 'now', no future, just 'now'.
For there is only the minute, your minute and your hour,
          preordained for you,
       for His will be done on earth,
             Now!

Part 4

New Life

An unlikely marriage came quite unexpectedly and, with it, my child Greg, a miracle in every sense. Because of our mutual desire not to be married in a Catholic church and the odd couple label somehow generated, we cancelled our wedding plans in a Church of England church and took ourselves to distant shores, namely South Africa.

Yes, I had met that South African family for a reason, which was now revealed. We were married in the sun-drenched living room of that dear friend, amidst a circle of unknowns, but uncertainty prevailed. Although our respective families had known one another through Catholic schooling since our arrival in the UK in 1960, paths rarely crossed.

Very soon in my pregnancy, bad news became a life-or-death decision. Our child had a hole in his diaphragm, and the option to terminate the pregnancy was offered. Many doctors explained the operation that would result, and chances of success were fifty-fifty. This hit me with such force that I capitulated under its weight and fell at the mercy of only one doctor willing to get off the fence and tell me what to do. He could see my pain and, without question, told me to proceed. Upon reflection, having a termination would not have been in the equation in any event, but we needed reassurance that a baby could survive the imminent surgery.

Knowing his gender long before his arrival gave us the chance to name him and speak to him quite literally. Strangely, one night in the pregnancy, I sat up abruptly in bed, having been told by a voice to call him Greg Alexander. From that very moment on, his name was chosen. I did not question the voice at the time but just thought it was a dream. It was a real audible voice.

Greg underwent a four-hour surgery performed by a doctor who had come especially from Guys Hospital in London. With eleven people in the delivery room awaiting Greg's arrival and in the full knowledge that this was not an ordinary baby, he was whisked away for immediate ventilation. If the lungs inflated on the first breath, all of the out-of-place organs would have caused havoc. Greg was thirty-six hours old when the knife slid across his miniature body and his insides were rearranged. His heart was in the right thoracic cavity, whilst the left lung was partial due to the fact that the stomach, kidneys, and spleen had all formed out of place. They all had to be handled and placed in their allotted spot. His intestines were handled, and his appendix was removed. Fortunately, there was adequate tissue around the diaphragm to obviate the need for the insertion of a patch. With insides rearranged, sewing the diaphragm was skillfully done, and the operation was deemed a success.

The hospital chapel had been my refuge during the long, agonizing hours of surgery, and I prayed incessantly. In order for vital organs to settle, it was necessary to sedate Greg thereafter, and a morphine drip was duly attached. It was not a pleasant sight, and I rarely left his side. During the delivery, my coccyx had been broken, and I too was hospitalized upstairs. Intensive care at the Bristol Maternity Hospital became my refuge and shelter. I stayed by Greg's side, sometimes through the night, praying for his recovery. It was not all smooth sailing, but dormant faith started to kick in. God's will was unfolding. I did not hold Greg for two weeks.

Before Greg's surgery, the vicar from my local church came into the hospital's ICU to baptize him, but I sensed this would not be necessary. He was going to survive and grow up normally. I thanked him but duly sent him away because I was convinced Greg would not only survive the operation but also pull through the early months.

However, warnings were still issued by concerned doctors who gently pointed out that

"In these sorts of cases, Mr. and Mrs. Polledri, it is usual for children to experience breathlessness in childhood …"

I took on board these warnings, with more fear being generated, but decided not to accept their unintended, yet divisive impact.

No immediate problems arose from the surgery, and Greg made a miraculous recovery. You would often find him balanced in the arms of the doctors doing the daily rounds, showing him off and singing his praises. Six weeks later, he was out of the hospital, heavily scarred, but well. That is all that mattered.

Now it needs to be pointed out that a much-loved child inside a precariously balanced, short marriage had to be managed and managed well. This was to be an only child. The marriage was not heaven orchestrated, but one that was manufactured and heavily laced in Catholic thinking.

For my husband, it was a second time around the block and, for him, a third child. Understandably his children of the former marriage did not welcome the fact that their beloved father had remarried after twelve years of singleness. Nor were they enamored by the introduction of a child at their dad's ripe old age of forty-seven years. For them, it was too much to bear, and resentment surfaced. After all, he had fought for them in a bitter divorce and won custody. He had married his life to them within the bosom of a close-knit Italian family, and grandparents had played the pivotal role throughout. In their minds, he was deserting them, and no mercy was shown. He was guilty as charged! Wagging tongues passed silent judgment, and frailty found the marriage strain a cozy retreat.

Years rumbled by, storm clouds regularly gathered, and lightning strikes were commonplace. We were not the run-of-the-mill family, and the opposing families never joined forces. We were married in name but not in soul and spirit. Were we two as one or two apart living the lie of one? Sadly, the latter assumed its role as key agitator, and the years saw an ever-broadening wasteland develop. We were poles apart, but our burdened Catholic consciences bid us remain together, as did the silent, sleeping partner, faith.

To escape our lie, we ran further and this time to the US. My husband was British, and his alien residency was eventually established. Greg, with his British birthright, also selected American citizenship. He was two years old, and we set up shop in Port Charlotte, Florida, feigning happiness for disapproving families left behind. My husband had bravely risen to the challenge of becoming an over-the-road driver, but his at-home record was poor. Moreover, the salary was abysmal and incapable of supporting a home and family, but his many trucking tales were worthy of note. They may even be the subject matter of a future book, for his experiences produced riveting, and captivating tales.

Just briefly imagine the scene if you can. A fifty year-old British-born, very pale, and balding Brit sent by his company on his first road trip to New York. He was a lamb to the slaughter for sure. His handle was Polar Bear. Add to this the bizarre tales from the Blue Ridge Mountains folk, mischievous to the point of sending a lost, inexperienced driver into a swamp, requiring a recovery wrecker to dislodge the eighteen-wheel beast, and the mind begins to boggle anew! Then being invited into a local wood cabin-style shack during his wait invokes further imaginings only matched by his vivid descriptions of the event on his return home. Couple this with the nightly truck stop service provided by known ladies of the night for lonely over-the-road truckers, of which he had no knowledge whatsoever, and the imagination is further invited to a feast of great magnitude. He was mercilessly teased and taunted by fellow truckers for such innocence.

Truck stop food, hmm. What could go amiss there? Well, a common language of English shared meant nothing. Ordering a large portion of chips was not exactly what he had in mind. French fries was the American terminology, and much laughter was enjoyed by those on his table seeing a mountain of potato chips arrive. And if an alligator on a road and a snake in the cab wasn't enough, then think of driving your eighteen-wheeler into an unseen, snow-clad car park of a maximum-security Chicago prison at night, having gone down the wrong side of the freeway to correct the mistake.

With sirens cutting into the cold, crisp night air and police surrounding his cab from all quarters, a scene that only movies can aptly paint, was fashioned. Gingerly stepping down from his cab with arms fully raised, he opened his mouth, and they listened. Strange lingo was his ultimate saving grace. Yes, he was telling the truth. The brutal winter storm had landed him into deep water or, should I say, deep snow. He was given a police escort back onto an open freeway and this time in the right direction. The Polar Bear was on the road again!

Let me get back from my brief detour. As I said earlier, the nature of the truck driver's life did not really lend itself to family life with a young child. The solution was returning to Bristol again. We left few tracks on the Florida shoreline but did retain priceless video footage of our little lad at Disney World; a bobcat running in the yard; Easter celebrations graced by a visit from my sister Patty, then living in Kingwood, Texas; and, of course, the requisite footage of a husband driving a humongous US truck.

During Greg's rising years, we spotted in him a sporting prowess to be admired. Whatever he put his mind to, he played well and with enormous flair and style. Cricket was his first love, followed by field hockey and tennis. Table tennis and snooker were close behind, and lurking in the background was a very raw, but very real, talent for golf. As parents, we both played. (Well, my husband played while I hacked around.) And Greg was always observing from afar. His father was a formidable sportsman to boast.

For my part, I decided to reclaim that legal qualification fought so very hard for years earlier and open a legal business. Professional telephone legal advice sold as an employee benefit was on my heart, and what started out as a passive vision became a twelve-year-long obsession. I wanted to establish a legal brand in the world, the first of its kind, so that people would and could access the law from one gateway. Professional help would be at the end of a telephone at the time of the need, and paid for by the employer.

Along with a silent partner, I founded and set up Telephone Legal Advice company from the confines of a small dining room in our two-bedroom flat. Greg was but three years old at the time, so he was still at my feet most of the day.

McDonald's is synonymous with hamburgers, Coca-Cola with soft drinks, and Kellogg's with cereals, so why couldn't my alternative legal company for professional telephone legal advice become an international brand? The company had only been up and running around twelve months when I received a telephone call from the Welfare Department of a prominent UK retailer no less. I was standing in my living room, clad in pink, fur-lined slippers, and speaking to them about my company, my baby, which shall remain unnamed for the present.

At the time, the company only had sixty-five private members, one corporate client, and one charity. This retailer had read a small article I had written in a charity's newsletter and wanted to meet.

Heaven-sent, was my immediate thought.

I duly attended a meeting with them at their head office in London. I should mention that my founding partner did not last the course for reasons of commercial good sense. Sadly, she was unable to see perspective other than from her own vantage point and vice versa, I suppose. We parted company at the insistence of an overbearing funding bank, and the door was sadly shut. Banks rule, right? I had no say. The company, my baby, continues to this day in the UK some twenty-three years on, and happily providing independent legal advice by telephone, for scores of needy individuals and companies.

Now, where was I? Greg. Sports. Golf! It was after one of our Easter trips to our time-share home in La Manga, Spain, that he began to display moderate interest in the game of golf. He was about eleven years old at the time, and while school sports still took precedence, he lifted the golf clubs when time permitted and the weather was kindly. Need I say, the temperamental English climate was not altogether obliging.

It was a slow but seductive start of a burning passion for the game, almost to obsession, and his wholehearted desire to try to obtain an American golf scholarship surfaced some five years later. The game was certainly not found on a UK's school curriculum as a rule, so the answer must lay some three thousand miles away in the US, or so we thought. But how do you move when you are in your fifties and sixties and your only child's life is bound in Bristol?

Were we making another journey into the unknown, or was God's perfect plan unfolding? We were clueless. We thought we were giving our son an opportunity of a lifetime. And with such reasoning firmly clenched in our fists, we prepared to move physically, unaware that hearts don't move quite so easily.

There was more turmoil for my mother and a huge upheaval from all we had established in England. The move to the US was final. We were repeating history, but unknowingly walking in His purpose. And for now, the end appeared to justify the means. Do we see what we think we see? Only the ending will reveal its mystery.

The Dark Light

How dark is the light we think we see
Enlightened world, how dark art thee?
Shrouded in light, the earthly kind,
Locked in squalor, O' enlightened mind!

Yet light there is in darkness too,
waiting to penetrate, enlightened you.
And free your soul, bedraggled heart
In Jesus's name, His light imparts.

But dark is the light we choose to see,

seducing the soul into eternity.
"Wake up, oh man, awake and be
the light in the dark, sweet sanity!"

Awaken now while time is kind
and not for you, be left behind.
But escape as through a fire, singed
dear rescued man, new life begins!

Part 5

Crunch Time!

Thoughts of our earlier, unsuccessful foray into US living, bobbed up and down in my mind, and gnawing, illogical thinking persisted. My position as founder and managing director of the legal company would have to be surrendered after a long twelve-year struggle but was timely. My heart insisted it was misplaced as managing director, and the withdrawal from my baby was put into motion. The company needed new direction, and it was time for me to step away gracefully. It was a heart-wrenching decision, but at least the US excuse afforded me a measure of dignity to step aside. This was to be shattered and ravaged by a duplicitous board. The darker and unsavory side of human nature was revealed among certain, once trusted colleagues, and I learned the meaning of shallowness personified.

I read every email exchanged among them months prior to my departure, and during the closing weeks and days, I read how deception was to be implemented, and the concept of honor for me was totally destroyed. The revelation was all too much for me to bear, and the arid offer of being retained as a non-executive director was a nonstarter. Cryptic emails had been sent behind closed doors, but of course through open windows.

A secret board meeting convened, and minutes were taken. It became an exercise of military precision, and their agreed strategy to ensure minimum money was paid out was activated. I had been betrayed, and I knew it firsthand. The silver pen handed to me over a paltry, leaving office lunch represented everything unholy in my mind.

I had read everything ... absolutely everything! I knew their hearts. I pitied them, but happily wounds have now healed, and forgiveness is complete. It's a glorious perspective to now be able to see both vantage points. Yet upon reflection, I am sure they were just behaving as any commercial entity would in all the circumstances, but I suspect I was too consumed with anger to even want to see or agree.

The move back to the US became imminent, and the town of Southlake, Texas, was our selected destination.

Why? I am sure you are thinking.

If you recall, many moons ago back in the 1970s, I had spent a couple years in Houston where long-standing friendships had been birthed. One of those friends was to be the dock and the anchor for our move. I was back in Texas thirty years on, this time with a husband and child in tow, as well as a fragile marriage.

I was the last to arrive in the US, and on November 20, 2006, I set my suitcase down once and for all, having completed seven return journeys earlier that year. I was tired, relieved, bruised, and anxious, but also inwardly steaming. The wounds inflicted by the company had penetrated deep, and I continued to delve into forbidden windows, eliciting yet more unsavory email exchanges. My mind justified the long-range intrusion and would have continued had not the hand of God reached down into my world and bid me to stop.

Christmas Eve 2006 saw upheaval in our house. It became all too much for my husband, and his strong family ties in the UK pulled his heartstrings. He was leaving. Bags were packed. Leaving. I was weary. I had loyally and faithfully stayed in the marriage, but if he wanted to return across the pond, then I was going to let him go. Again, the good Lord, whom I really did not know at the time, stepped in to salvage the sinking ship.

Only a month before, we had met a wonderful man named Barry while standing in a local computer shop. He immediately befriended us and introduced us to his circle of friends. It was to this man that I turned on this particular Christmas Eve and revealed my husband's anxieties, and intentions.

At two o'clock on that day and accompanied by Gary, another warrior, they came to the rescue. Scooping my confused husband into their arms and whisking him away for over four hours, they reached into his doubts, encouraged him, and prayed for him, and he was returned with a changed mind. God certainly worked at an almighty pace that Christmas Eve.

An invisible plan was being put in place. It was still a strain for us all, particularly my son, who could not fathom what was happening, but our presence in Texas was not by chance or choice. It was a divine appointment of which we knew nothing at the time, but would be revealed just thirty days later. Isn't it great that we don't know what is going to happen from one minute to the next?

These friends, or perhaps I should call them angels, organized that my husband attend a men's retreat in the Texas Hill Country. Its purpose was explained, but its meaning did not even touch the surface of my cognizant thinking. As far as I was concerned, he would be out of my hair for five days, and I would have some time to reflect. I too needed space.

His return certainly reflected change in his aura, and his temper most definitely had been rearranged and assuaged. However, I remained suspicious, cynical in fact, for I knew the nature of the beast with whom I was dealing. He declared that he had found God and been born again. Oh no, not that *born-again* term that I hotly despised, but I would bide my time and hold my tongue once again. I had been doing it for sixteen years, so why change the pattern?

My son carefully observed his every action and word upon his return, as did I. "Practice what you preach" became our mantra, and we watched. If the marriage was going to survive and my sanity remain intact, it was a prerequisite that I too attend this mysterious rendezvous point in Southern Texas. I was not particularly receptive to the idea, but neither was I hostile to its invitation. I decided that a marriage had to be fought for, even unwillingly, and I acquiesced to my reservation being made just thirty days later.

Oh, sweet timing, Lord. You have everything under control,

but I was not aware of this. After all, God, you were elusive, distant, unreachable, and reserved for Sundays only as far as my psyche was concerned. But you drew me in a way that could and can only be done by your invisible yet invincible power. I was to be tested in the furnace, released from my lifetime shackles, and freed from that open prison. I was to be saved and born again, but I knew not!

So I too made the journey to the Hill Country of Southern Texas where my husband had just been, and I was to be in the company of sixteen ladies who were complete strangers to me. With disinterest and a measure of hostility, I unenthusiastically packed a bag, and with hidden cynicism and resentment, I departed for the unknown.

The title of this book was not one of choice or intellectual process. It was quite literally spoken to me on the evening of March 8, 2007, and as you read further, you will see that *Your Life in My Hands* is my testimony and His will. Should it touch a single heart this side of heaven and that heart then reaches out to another, then the kingdom surely comes, and His will is most certainly done.

What follows is a detailed account of the trip and my life after that divine appointment covering some ten years up to present day. I was born again. I was becoming a new creation in Jesus Christ, and I am His child, forgiven and free!

Travel with me now and see God's hand at work. Observe His power! Believe His purpose, and receive His love. He is on every page, and He is speaking to you! Let's go!

Chapter 1

Thursday, Day 1

When boarding a bus called *Fellowship of the Sword* with fifty-three years of life tightly entwined around your body, strangling the very breath out of you, agitating with years inside an empty marriage, and having childhood memories bobbing up and down in tune with the tapestry of youth's promiscuity, the prognosis for the trip does not seem good. You believe that your past is immeasurably worse than those sitting all around you, and you shrink back into your seat, anticipating the worst.

I was on a bus bound for a ranch in a location I knew not, but somewhere in the Hill Country of Southern Texas. That's all I really knew or cared to understand. I had reached the end of the road in terms of the designer lifestyle I had created with all its pitfalls, and I wanted my life back. I had died a slow death inside, and it was my time to see, to be born again.

While sitting shoulder to shoulder amidst total strangers, stories unfold before your very eyes, and the fallen world's lives reveal abhorrent truths and cruel realities. You then realize that you are not alone, and the common ingredient shared is bondage, all courtesy of captive free will. Bound we were, but soon to be loosed.

Shackled to the very tips of our heads by life's inequities, I embarked on a journey of apparent darkness, only rivaled by the compelling light it would shed upon my return to reality five days later. But for now, it was an unknown, and I sat nervously, knowing that soon it would be my turn to disclose and spill all. It would be my turn to tell my unabridged story to persons I had never set eyes on before, driver included.

You see, you have the choice. You have center stage. Come clean, and be rid of the gangrene-infested memory bank that continues to deprive you of life, bind, and gag you, all courtesy of the ever-present and resident accomplice, the devil, or you can hold back and justify your stance. It's your choice after all, and captive free will is the common denominator. I chose to conform!

For some, it was all too much, and life's horror stories were screened without censor to an unsuspecting audience. Reality hits hard, tears well up, and your heart bleeds as you listen incredulously to life's victims. Taken by surprise, you begin to see a pattern of merciless subjugation experienced by so many and at the hands of those trusted most. It's life's irony at its best.

For many, bitterness took root, and un-forgiveness became a justified means to an end; the due punishment for those who relentlessly had tormented and tortured a life just to gratify sadistic cravings or power-hungry appetites. Those who had fallen foul and who had fouled sat pensively, nervously awaiting their airtime.

Longing for peace, release from captive pasts, and the freedom to lay claim to promised futures, we tarry a while longer, wondering and doubting the outcome. Detours will be shelved for five days at least, and the small gate with a narrow road beyond is illuminated.

The five-hour journey passed with the blink of an eye, but its cutting-edge technology of purpose deeply incised my very soul. I was speechless within but feigned the talk, heavily masked. I knew my time would come to reveal all. The arrival at the ranch provided me with some temporary respite, only to discover that my time to confess was ahead.

Off the bus and in the ranch, it was called a *mercy seat*, a term I had never encountered, but an essential throne where the sordid of life is revealed and unwelcome thoughts, deeds, and words are confessed, declared, and thereafter put to death.

I bore my soul at two in the morning on March 2, 2007, on

my mercy seat and in the company of total strangers. My salvation was proclaimed! I had been a Catholic for a lifetime, so I naturally thought I was already a member of the club. I was a Catholic after all, so I must have been saved! My infant baptism, first holy communion, and early confirmation bore witness to the fact, but had my life to that point reflected the glories of our Creator and Savior? Or did they sadly reflect another whom we all know but perhaps choose to ignore too readily and almost incessantly? For now, salvation was the requisite first step on what was going to be a fierce battle for my release into His freedom.

Salvation was secured. A strange bed was a welcome refuge from unimaginable beginnings. And to think I had unwittingly boarded a bus just hours earlier, angry, skeptical, and blissfully unaware of what lay ahead. Oh, sweet mercies! He's in control for sure!

At the point of being emotionally drained, my selected perch gave temporary rest to an already weary traveler, and the evening closed. Did dreams accompany my night hours? No, I was in His peace.

Chapter 2

Friday, Day 2

As the new day gave witness to yesterday's truths, the well-prepared manuals provided by the retreat staff (and I can now say unwaveringly that they were written by heaven's pen) were distributed and opened. God's divine appointments were to be set in motion.

There was no turning back. Four thousand miles away from my recently departed home in Bristol, England, I was sitting midst a sea of uncertainty, surrounded by a cocktail of love's pylons and many crumbling columns. What was happening? Why was I there?

I donned my mask of confidence and entered into the arena once more. Breakfast had been fastidiously prepared by willing volunteers clothed in rich humility and ready to serve as love's wrap to a battered brood. I knew in my innermost being that it was time to face up to the miserable and pitiful existence that I had with open eyes devised, maneuvered, manipulated, steered, and accepted for a lifetime. Oh, I was so presentable on the outside, but on the inside, I was just a decaying mass, the stench of which our fearless friend, the skunk, would welcome into his armory.

Only two days prior to my departure, I had felt the desperation of life's cumulating circumstances converge into one horrible mass, and I reached rock bottom. I had broken down before an unsuspecting Bible study group. (How clever my disguise had been since I arrived in the US.) And I sobbed bitter tears. I had somehow let myself slither and slide into the deepest pit where only slender rays of opaque light could penetrate. The word *transparent* was given to a lady to give to me, which meant nothing whatsoever to me at the time, but today I know I was being prepared for my appointment with the Almighty!

The first full day at the ranch somewhere in Southern Texas was relaxed and reassuring. A gracious family had donated it for this specific use, and what a blessing it had been to so many thus far. Lives were freed through another's selfless generosity. I was bowled over to think that such people existed, and I was to become part of the blessing bestowed.

You know, it is said that God works in mysterious ways, and this was one of them. I don't suppose for one moment that the owners envisaged upping sticks one day, moving out of the area, and handing over the keys to what was indisputably an expensive piece of real estate, but that is just what they did. Thank you, whoever you are. Our Almighty Father knows!

To continue, our planned schedule was contained in specially prepared manuals, and we got started. One task was to decorate a box.

Hmmm, my worst nightmare, I thought.

Playing with glue, sequins, paints, and all other artistic paraphernalia was, for me, a big no-no. I could not think of anything worse than spending time designing a box, the purpose of which was not revealed. Instructions were clear. Decorate it however you wanted to, but make sure it was finished and ready for show by six o'clock on Monday night.

What did all this mean? I thought.

I begrudgingly stepped into what looked like an arts and crafts class, donned my "Oh, isn't this fun" mask, and commenced. Without too much thought at all, I was somehow clearly led to design a ladder into the stars with moon adjacent. The sky was scattered with sparkle, and the names of my husband and son were included. I had very little patience for this type of activity, but I soon discovered the joy was derived from talking with fellow questers. Colorful characters were unveiling yet more truths, while exhibiting obvious artistic flair. It was fun, and its purpose would be revealed on the final evening. How? I hadn't a clue!

I now know this was the lull before the storm, but I didn't realize that at the time. I felt secure away from my humdrum existence and relieved to be released. I was sharing a room with three complete strangers in close quarters, but I felt okay. They had suffered the indignities of life's menu and were also searching for that heavenly key, freedom. Our common denominator bound us without limitation, and we blended as well as any blender could concoct.

Chance? I think not. Again divine appointments were set in motion for us all and without exception. No stones had been left unturned the night before, so cards were on the table. And the most personal of detail had been divulged. We could be without worry. That's freedom!

I cannot say I felt the Lord's presence the second day as much as I tried to still myself, listen, and follow their instructions, but I do recall a very real sense of security and an overwhelming knowing on the part of those who served us so selflessly. No head was hung in shame, and you could be 'you' whoever that was.

We had all come together as a motley crew with true-life stories that would put Hollywood to task with all its decadence, gratuitous violence, and decaying themes, mass-produced today for maximum profit and benefit. Our scripts, you see, were real with no editing or choreography. They had been raw impact without censor. They were real stories from breaking hearts, some that had already been broken over and over again but soon to be overhauled and made new. Thank God.

I walked through the day somewhat in a daze. Although salvation had been proclaimed and life's miscellany of masks discarded, peace still eluded me. In between the arts and crafts lesson, I found myself adorning the mercy seat several times that day as past sins flooded to the forefront of my mind, were publicly confessed, dealt with, and cast out. Repentance was not just a question of feeling guilty and saying "sorry." It was more than that. It was the relentless pursuit of my heart by God through his Holy Spirit and His Son Jesus.

And what of my heart? It had become a hardened mass of fear that had played hostess to the black widow for a lifetime and was soon to be released from its tormentor. I had swallowed the lie and even believed its disguised truths. I had been an integral part of the affluent poor, strutting upon the stage and playing my part, unaware that it was leading me blindfolded into a place of no return, yes, hell, with all its miseries and hopelessness. That is where I was heading, and I didn't even know it. I thought I was respectable and hardworking. I was a mother, a wife, a daughter, an aunt, and even a great-aunt. I had been blinkered and deceived. Now I was saved!

The day revealed salutary facts about the next day's activity, simply described as a day of fasting and silence in the wilderness. The idea of it conjured up all sorts of images in my mind and aroused mixed emotions. I listened attentively to all the instructions, but somehow my consciousness did not register what our volunteer servers were saying. There was no food, no talking, and no makeup. It was just the wilderness and me, or so I thought. It was my day to find God. It was my day to be found!

Chapter 3

Saturday, Day 3

The morning arrived, and the prior evening's instructions were meticulously followed. It was a day of fasting, silence, and release into the wilderness at regular intervals. The day before had seen the sun release a welcome warmth for a March day, but today, although the sun shone brightly, the easterly wind blew. Cold and chilling, it knew its diversionary power. Business was about to begin in earnest. What mayhem must have reigned in the heavenly realms that morning as the forces of good and evil prepared to do battle over our wilderness souls. I had read that our battle was not against flesh and blood, but against the rulers, authorities, and powers of our dark world and the spiritual forces of evil in the heavenly realms.

To that point, I had never taken on board or bothered to take on board what it meant. They were just words in the Bible that I had skimmed over time and time again. Little did I know that this day would change my life and reveal to me the poignancy of those oft-read but misunderstood Bible verses. Little did I know their power!

With a knapsack on my back laden with water bottles, Bible, and manual; a fold-up chair underarm; and warm hat in hand, I left the warmth and security of the ranch and headed out. But where? What was I expecting to see or hear out there in the remote five hundred acres? Yes, livestock formed part of the terrain, as did birds and the foliage, but the Maker of the Universe, where would He be? What form would He take?

I tenaciously headed toward the gates, negotiating the cattle grid's intricacies, and walked ahead. I had been told to ask where I should go, but what did that mean? The mind can play such wonderful tricks. My first attempt at finding a place of solitude resulted in an about-turn and the call to a riverside location. The Guadalupe River spread its history through this ranch, and after a twenty-minute walk, I settled beneath the shelter of a tree amidst the riverbank's swaying reeds. The gentle sound of the river trickled past as the sun beat its glory through the ever-prevailing and cutting easterly wind. I tried to settle myself by praying and talking, completing the exercises that had been set within our manuals, while fidgeting and waiting. But what exactly was I waiting for or expecting? Not a clue!

I strained to hear, see signs, and listen for the unusual, but instead a sea of emotions drowned me, and tear-spotted pages started to assemble before me. I began to verbally spew out my loathsome past, and shameful thoughts clad me from head to toe. I cried out loud uncontrollably. Invaded by emotions, frustration surged.

Where was He? I don't hear Him! What was I expecting? I can't see Him.

After four hours, I decided to reposition myself. Nothing appeared to be happening apart from a torrent of tears.

Maybe if I move, He will be there!

I repacked my knapsack and walked down the road alongside the river. It was open, the sun shone, and I perched upon open, flat rock. I imagined snakes and saw only stones.

I need not fear, need I?

Another hour passed, and I waited. There was silence! Again, I resumed my quest back down the road from whence I had come and stepped off the private road and into an open, grassy patch that straddled the river. I complained aloud that I did not know where I should sit as I walked back and forth surveying the terrain. Without warning, the strap of my knapsack cut sharply into my shoulder, and I sensed I should stop immediately, be still, and wait. I obeyed.

Unpacking the chair, I placed it down indiscriminately,

although I did ensure the sun was shining on that particular corner. Birds darted from tree to tree, and the ever-present sound of the Guadalupe orchestrated the background.

Now what?

There were passages to read from the manual, and the proposed timetable had by now been abandoned. I seemed to be running at least an hour behind schedule, but I soldiered on. Some thirty-two scriptures, a sentence or two only, covered the next two pages. I read through each one, as instructed, but nothing happened. They were just empty words.

At the end, two questions were posed: "Were these verses comforting to you? Did they wrap around you like a warm blanket, or did they leave you feeling cold?"

As frustrations mounted, the dormant volcano within me exploded, and I yelled out loud, "No, they didn't comfort me. They didn't comfort me at all. I feel cold. I feel cold to the bone, and I feel alone. I don't feel your presence. No, they don't comfort me at all!"

My head then sunk into my icy palms, and I sobbed bitterly. What was happening? As my tears filled my hands and my nose became a streaming river, an audible voice loudly proclaimed, "Hear it now! Hear it now! Hear it now!"

I slowly turned to my left to determine the speaker, and thereby perched on low-hanging branches were birds watching me and speaking. Was I going absolutely crazy?

I know birds don't talk. They only sing, don't they?

"Hear it now! Hear it now! Hear it now!" reverberated through the crisp air.

I understood. He was there. He was trying to get my attention. This He did in one swift action, and I succumbed. I cannot accurately describe the minutes that followed, but I pressed forward, knowing. I obeyed for once in my life without using common sense or logical thoughts.

The next instructions in what was described as our Wilderness Day manual were a welcome sight for sore eyes. "Find a comfortable spot and take a nap."

Whoopee! I felt emotionally drained and bedazzled by the previous minutes' encounter. I dutifully laid my head back on the seat and closed my eyes to let the sun shine upon a weary soldier. As I relaxed, I felt a very sharp tug on my hair, and I quickly turned around to look and see the identity of the culprit. I had assumed it was a fellow quester playing a prank. Expecting to see a face, I sat openmouthed, staring at nothingness, just trees.

The yank of my hair had been so strong that I interpreted this as the Father telling me to keep going, another sign from Him. Only today I know different. It was not Him that hurt me, but that pesky, rotten devil. One of His most treasured possessions was being removed from His clenches, and He was not going to let me go without a fight. I was oblivious to it all, and I was now fair game in that spiritual realm.

Slowly I began to feel as though I was in some kind of unseen battle. I cannot adequately describe the uncharacteristic unease that invaded my body, but I was not happy. The next minute, I found myself prostrate against the cold earth, repenting and crying out for all the pain I had caused others and for having been such a miserable sinner. My past alcoholic bouts had loosed my tongue to such an extent that I had dealt fatal blows to many unsuspecting souls and enacted the debauch behavior it had produced. I repented over and over.

Moments later I found myself sitting upright, composed, and responding to the manual. Except my response did not correspond to the instructions. Instead I was frantically penning verses that poured out of my being, and these I give to you exactly as they were penned, without alteration. These were His words, bearing witness to my battle as it continued to rage.

> Out of the darkness I crawled,
> all battered, bruised, dirty.
> Shame clothed me, and I wept.
> The light shone upon a weary traveler,
> and I broke into a million pieces.

He yanked and pulled; I kept slipping.
His love stood firm and held on tightly.
My condemnation cape was swiftly removed,
and there exposed vulnerability,
sorrow, pain, shame, hurt, gushing
forth like the river torrents.
And so the journey started with
new clothes and empty cases
surrounded by heaven's hosts.

As I stumbled, He held me firm.
As I crashed down again, the heavenly
realms upheld me.
As I endured, He carried me.

He made His light shine upon
me, all new and glowing,
safe, secure, purposeful in love.
My sorrows had subsided, and my pains healed.
I cried; He answered and said

"Come, lovely daughter, let's walk
a while; let's talk a while.
Let's get to know each other.
Shall we dance on a bright, joyous daytime?
Let me wrap my arms around you and
show you the universe, My world.
Your life in My hands.
Shall we dance?"

As I hurriedly scribbled down these verses, I stopped, read them, and then questioned their author. Yes, I had physically written them down, but did I compose them in three short minutes?

The time was marching on, and my mind had become a tangled

mass of fact and fiction. I cannot honestly say either that I felt the joy that so many others had experienced in their search for God, for my inquiring mind would still not permit me to believe. I remained shackled, for I had to find a rational explanation for talking birds and unintended poetry. I had to know who or what had tugged at my hair and why my knapsack had become so weighty as to force me to stop dead in my tracks. Nothing made sense, and I needed to find rational explanations.

I was a businesswoman, and I had come to the US to re-establish an American branch of the English operation I had founded some ten years earlier. After all, that was one of the reasons for my moving to Texas, having just spent a lifetime in the UK, wasn't it? I was a lawyer by profession (but non-practicing) and an ex-managing director of the company I had founded.

In my early twenties and thirties, I had travelled the world and stayed at the finest hotels. I had drunk copious amounts of the finest wines and champagnes and indulged in the Babylonian lifestyle of chauffeur-driven cars and private Citation II jet travel. I had first-class travel, designer clothes, Puerto Banus holidays with its attendant debauchery, and endless nights spent in Marbella's finest nightclub amidst the world's jet-setters. Bimini, Cat Cay, London, Paris, Monte Carlo, Nice, Cannes, Madrid, and Cape Town had been my haunts that had played host to my folly.

Now the hour had already reached five thirty, and I headed back to reality, the safe haven of the ranch. The volunteer angels had welcomed us back with much-needed warm soup, but silence remained part of the fast. I know I had misunderstood the instructions today. I had assumed we could talk aloud to God, but no. Happily I also know today that He knew my heart and I was not being openly defiant. I just had not listened to the instructions carefully. How unusual! Do we ever listen?

We concluded the evening together and shared our experiences. I listened to the many riveting accounts of encounters with God or brushes with the other, but I still felt ill at ease. Mine had been a battle. Could I possibly declare that I had heard birds talking, my hair had been physically pulled, and words from up above had been downloaded into my pen? Would they believe or think I had been hallucinating? Again I was the very last person to recall the day's events.

These were duly revealed, and the poem was read. Silence filled the air as my fellow questers listened and absorbed a divine appointment enacted. The evening drew to a conclusive end. God was moving.

Chapter 4

Sunday, Day 4

The previous day's memories were still fresh in my mind as we gathered together for a hearty breakfast. Life's company of optimists and pessimists had been thrown together like stir-fry ingredients, tossed, stirred, and served. It was a feast to behold and carefully blended together by its sky chef. This sounds a trifle bizarre, but the speed at which complete strangers came together, divulged the most personal of details, and served them à la carte struck me as out of the ordinary. This wasn't a coincidence of life's circumstances that could be reasoned away. This was different. This was God's plan for us.

I trod carefully from breakfast to lunch, participating in the planned sessions, observing, and waiting. I did not feel particularly settled, and during a midday talk, I was told very boldly to tell the ladies that they were about to go out into Heartbreak Canyon. The words had no meaning whatsoever to me, but I duly delivered the message, sensing my obligation, and slumped back into the room's easy chairs.

For some of you reading this, you may be thinking, *What? Who told her and how?*

I can only say a voice from within made it clear. It was unrelated to a video talk we had just watched and quite off the wall in context, so I can only tell you how it was. It didn't make any sense at all to me, but I delivered.

The afternoon's instructions were then sensitively handed out, and in our own time, we set out individually to spend more time alone. Stepping out into the midday sunshine, unencumbered and free to be, we intermittently left the ranch. Some found their quiet spot almost immediately, while others did not. I strolled along, soaking up the warm, midday sunshine, and purposefully headed toward the heart of the ranch, but this time away from the pleasant distraction of the Guadalupe River, I needed to be in isolation without distraction. I strolled past the stables and corral, observed the cattle observing me, and then disappeared into the brush. I must admit the thought of snakes befell me. I had been told that Texas was home to a variety, so I watched my step. I seemed to walk for at least twenty minutes, scaling walls and shimmying under barbed wire fences. A stench most foul wafted past my unsuspecting nose, and there in the distance laid the rotting carcass of a head of cattle. I promptly turned at a 180-degree angle and walked in the opposite direction. It was a depressing sight, which I suppose had been arranged for me, but I paid little time pondering and carried on. That is how I would have ended up, a rotting, decaying mass had it not been for love's intervention.

It wasn't long before I found a clearing with some interesting white rocks that looked like the perfect place to perch my bottom. Again thoughts of snakes plagued me, and the requisite hissing noise resounded as I settled down. I purposely ignored them as they had surely been put there for my fear-filled distraction.

It was a time of quiet reflection, followed by what appeared to be a question-and-answer session. A strike on my shoulder from behind sharply interrupted my initial peace. I swiftly turned to determine the deliverer but soon realized its source. I was slightly unnerved but thought I must keep going. I was in a safe place after all and guarded by the Maker of the Universe. What could such insignificance really do other than cause aggravation? Stir that fear! I was no longer the victim, and I had the victory, so I rather childishly told the tormentor to go away. I wasn't as polite as that, but the message was spoken and received.

The sun drenched my perch, and I felt warm to the heart. For over three hours, we spoke. I think I spoke most of the time, typical of my controlling personality, and sometimes I even listened. Over and over in my mind, I replayed yesterday's events, half expecting a visitation but accepting peace, apart from the unpleasant strike on my shoulder.

When I felt it time to return to the ranch, I casually gazed down at the ground, only to discover that I had been sitting on a red ant's nest. Thousands of them laid claim to my perch as I gently arose, and dread filled my heart. Only the day before had I heard horror stories from fellow questers who had fallen foul of these pesky creature's tactics, so much so that clothing had had to be removed.

I was expecting the same fate. Believe it or not, the stone was covered from the ground up and over, but not one red ant was found on my clothing, shoes, or being. I was in the middle of an ant's nest, and I had been left alone. I was more than taken aback and realized that this was not just a fluke or bit of good fortune. It was a divine appointment that could not be spoiled by anyone or anything whatever.

The more I reflect upon that incident, the more I realize that it was a miracle and there is no other explanation. Red ants normally show no mercy, but today God's hand completely covered me, and nothing could penetrate its shield.

I composed myself, gave huge thanks to that invisible helper, and left. I was not completely calm as I had once again felt the attack of the not so friendly, invisible thing, but I put those thoughts to one side, retraced my steps, and headed back to our collective, physical shelter of the ranch.

En route back, I had the excellent fortune of walking straight into some real cowboys, just fixin' to go riding. A pleasant English girl was among them, whom I discovered was the wife of one of the cowboys. She loved living in the US and the Texan lifestyle. She was horse crazy, so it must have been seventh heaven living and working on this sort of ranch with show horses just yards behind, away from visitor's glares. I was told they were magnificent specimens, as one was proudly led out of his stable and into the corral for exercise. I saw a Peruvian stallion, feisty and definitely nervous of strangers like me.

Doubtless, it sensed my own fear of horses. I was invited to observe the training, which I duly did. I now understand people's passion for horses. They are regal creatures, sure-footed and powerful.

Conscious of the time, I bid my farewell and left. I felt a kind of thrill overwhelm me as I strolled away. It didn't make sense, but I felt almost privileged to see firsthand the prized horses that we had all been politely told were off-limits and out of bounds. We could go anywhere on the ranch, but we were not to go into those stables. They housed the owner's treasured possessions and could be easily upset.

This, of course, reminded me of Adam and Eve's plight. Do and eat whatever you want, but don't eat from that tree! It will cause you problems if you do! That was a simple and fair instruction from their benefactor, so why the problem? I suspect we all know the answer. We want to have it our way and no other. Look where we are today. Confusion reigns while evil luxuriates among Earth's willing adherents to the "My Will Be Done Club."

By the way, I had been a lifetime member up until three days earlier, but my membership was now permanently cancelled. I know I would continue to receive reminder notices, enticing me to rejoin with all sorts of free offers, but I also know how to respond this time. Reject and discard immediately, and if the occasional mailer gets through, review, repent, and start again. There's no other way. Head for that mercy seat hastily!

Returning from Heartbreak Canyon, I stole myself away to walk around the house while last-minute preparations for supper were in hand. We were well nourished in more ways than I can explain, but mealtimes engendered camaraderie extraordinaire, the likes of which I had not in my lifetime encountered. We were sisters, the best of friends, and soul mates, all in a matter of four short, action-packed days. What was happening?

After the evening feast was enjoyed—and fine fare it was—we

all retired to the main living room to reveal to one another the day's manifestations and stories. It had become a special time for us where invisible bonding was taking place and love's knot was tied. The mercy seat was also given pride of place for those of us who were prompted to further cleanse their house, and I obediently took my turn. The buried past had been radically excavated only the day before, but residual debris clung tightly, resisting all attempts at removal.

I calmly recalled the day's events to my loyal sisters until a tide of emotion welled up without warning, and tears flowed mercilessly of tsunami proportions. Where did that come from? Could there really be anything left inside the empty cavern to reveal and remove? Yes, plenty!

A battle began to rage within, and the cold, steely glare of a prowling lion's eyes locked onto me. The chase was on. I was the prey, and the predator had me within his sight. He intended to seize me by the jugular and tear me to shreds if I let him. But I knew, by making a clean break from all that held me in his line of vision, that was my escape route. Without hesitation, I continued to bare my soul to my earthly and heavenly witnesses, all the while forging a way ahead to freedom.

Moments later, as I raised my head and disengaged from inexplicable phenomena, I returned to my chair shaken and listened in silence to my new sisters' testimonies. The spotlight had shifted, and I was, for then at least, finished.

The evening was rounded off with music to soothe the soul and to which all were invited to respond in ways our hearts directed. My heart felt robbed of its passion, or so I thought, listless and weary, and I participated in body only.

A tap on my shoulder from the facilitator brought me to my senses, and she asked whether I wanted to be baptized along with my fellow quester who too had been saved on March 2, 2007. We had spoken about my Catholic infant baptism earlier and the fact that water baptism was fundamental to the ongoing process of new life.

I wholeheartedly agreed, and plans were set in motion for baptisms in an appropriate place.

The March cold air and the temperature of the swimming pool dictated the location of the baptism. It was not to be outside. (Thank the Lord!) There were not only one or two, but five ladies who stepped forth seeking water baptism. For each, it was to be a personal experience but, most importantly, the removal of yet another shackle. Freedom was being set free, if that makes any sense to you, and gradually life's layers—inequities, rivalry, pains, and shames—were peeled away, and glory was being installed. New life was born. To many, you will think these are just words, but to me, they were and are life-changing. When you meet the Maker of the Universe, you tend to sit up and obey. Believe me! You do!

After the excitement of the day, the baptisms, and photography bearing witness to new lives resurfacing, sleep was a welcome retreat into which I wholeheartedly surrendered. Playing possum was no longer a part of my life's game plan. It had been fired. I was born again!

Chapter 5

Monday, Day 5

As Monday dawned and another day stretched out before us, my thoughts began to entertain doubt. What more could we possibly do or expect to receive? I had just been baptized, and the weekend had, for me at least, been one almighty struggle as the battle for my release raged. I felt physically tired and mentally drained. Voices befuddled my thus far untrained mind, and I now began to plummet into unchartered territories. How could this be?

Years and years of life's best-kept secrets spilt forth without warning, but residual, painful thoughts still filled my mind to capacity. I had understood that my past had been forgiven, but its reality had not yet bitten. What did that mean, and how would it show itself? Weren't my sins washed clean only the night before, or so I thought?

One of the ladies in the room discerned my discomfort. Her knowledge of the Bible was extraordinary. She walked and talked me through the many large question marks I had. Her testimony had been particularly grueling, one of those uncensored scripts that caught me in left field, and her meeting with our Creator had come almost seventeen years earlier. She had been where I was now and could speak with reassuring love and authority. I respected her from the minute we met, and today I can call her my "sister in Christ." We are friends, and we understand that privilege.

The afternoon's session comprised a televised talk by the founder of Fellowship of the Sword, and it offered the perfect ingredients, some light comic relief mixed with sound biblical teaching. As she related many of her own personal experiences to us, she said, almost word for word, the message I had been asked to tell the ladies only the day before, Heartbreak Canyon and so on.

There was a look of shock on many of the ladies' faces as the words emerged from her mouth. Many stared at me and smiled. Déjà vu filled their hearts, and I too felt the strangest sensation cascading within. It was almost eerie in its effect, and I did not know how to respond. Was it prophecy? No, prophecy was something that happened a couple thousand years ago. And who was I anyway? The incident caused much talk among my sisters, and I knew that something weird and wonderful was happening.

I had said those same words myself, and I had been convicted to open my once, firmly closed mouth and speak aloud a message. Today I believe it was the Holy Spirit's way of telling me, "Yes, Pamela, you do understand. You do get it, and you're caught. Now don't wrestle and try to get loose any more. You are mine. You were bought at a price, and I want you to stay close and know that I am!"

I spent the rest of the day in anticipation of a special evening that had been planned for us, the details of which were carefully kept secret, but we were assured we would enjoy. We had been asked to bring one special outfit, and tonight was the time to produce the glad rags and shine.

I must confess that, when I set off only four days earlier, the thought of dressing up and putting on yet another ball gown had not thrilled me, and I only packed something presentable to wear. I did not want to play ball, so I acquiesced to the degree I was willing to. And today I can say that I was the loser. I felt underdressed when I saw the majority of ladies step out in beautiful, chic dresses adorning glittering jewelry and hosting beaming smiles. He has been oh so patient with me.

We all assembled in the main living room, and as the ladies entered intermittently, you could hear the sighs of dismay and visual displays of joy as otherwise burdened travelers entered, transformed into beautiful princesses. Our plainness had been transformed into radiance, each lady with her own special appeal. Having attended so many functions in the past and having dressed the part oh so many times, I was slightly reticent about the whole evening. I could see I was underdressed, and I knew my pre-arrival attitude had been less than wholesome, but the enemy knew exactly where the weaknesses remained, and he locked in on them swiftly. I too recognized his gait, and I sidestepped his lock and entered the arena without too much fear.

We had been told to bring our boxes. All would be revealed. I cannot divulge any further detail, but suffice to say, purpose was well grounded. We assembled in the hallway where a table had been laid with pre-dinner nibbles and our boxes in hand. There was an air of excitement, which was further added to as two, extremely handsome, clean-cut, and well-groomed cowboys entered into the hallway. I was taken aback because this was an all-female affair and I didn't know cowboys cleaned up so well. They were absolutely charming and courteous to a fault. You will recall that I had met one of them just the day before at the corral.

Again, I must hold back the reason for their presence, but should you ever decide one day to make your pilgrimage to this remote ranch in Southern Texas—and I know Bunyan would be chuffed to bits for he loves pilgrims—there to meet your Maker, you too will share the experience. I am praying for that day for you, dear reader.

The evening's finale was a night of surprises, indulgence, pampering, and revelation. I became acutely aware of the past day's experiences, along with their impact and meaning for my life. Again, I cannot openly share the content of the evening with you, for I am prayerful that some of you who read this testimony will also open the doors of your heart, step outside, and find yourself as only you can within the confines of God's rendezvous location, wherever that may be. Let's just say that the evening was a blessing!

Chapter 6

Tuesday, Day 6

The following morning promised some free time, but also obligation. It was time to leave the security of the ranch, and head back to your own personal reality. We had to clean the house from floor to ceiling before departure and in preparation for the next incumbents. Some chose to savor the last few hours outdoors amidst the wilderness, while others busied themselves, packing and mingling. I think I was the latter. However, one fellow quester returned to the house with her demeanor ruffled and her message clear. Someone among us had not gotten it!

Got what? I thought.

Someone was going to leave in compromise, and whoever it was, she was to stop, reflect, and ask again where the strongholds lay. As she uttered the words, my emotions overtook me, and I hurriedly left the kitchen and headed for my bedroom. My roommates respected the solitude I needed and left the room. I was alone.

Was it me that had not gotten it? I thought.

As I sat with my head deeply buried in my hands, loud music started to play from the wall right next to me with the words, "You can dance. You can dance, having the time of your life …" resounding throughout the room. I was taken aback, and there was no explanation other than the Creator had reached down into the room to shake me, to wake me and to further engage me.

Logic took its place, and I sought a reason for the music's source. And no, there was no human reason to explain the miracle. It was just that, a miracle and a desperate plea to me to fully surrender and believe. There was no turning back. I had been told to "Hear it now" three times, and my time for miracles was upon me. I proceeded to pray with four of the volunteer angels and explained the music sounding forth from the bedroom wall. They understood, but at that point, I really didn't.

A battle of extreme proportions ensued with the enemy's penetrating eyes locked firmly onto me. As clear as I see, before me appeared a black steel wall and what looked like windows with black bars on each side. I was in a prison cell. As I stared at the dark wall, the two eyes fixed on me. He, Satan, was not going to let me go!

I began to panic, and I cried out for peace. How could I penetrate the wall? How could I be freed? Why was the barrier so stark? What seemed like ten to fifteen minutes of nonstop prayer passed, and after what seemed an eternity, the wall fell, the eyes disappeared, and serenity was embodied in what was an awesome-colored blue eye and dark eyebrows. Had I just had a glimpse of the Father? Yes, I had, and to that, I will add nothing further. I was at last free. It was my time for miracles. It was my release time.

Forces beyond my knowledge and understanding had consumed me, but now I had surrendered my all and was free to walk. I was now better prepared for the journey to my eternal home and equipped to do battle. I no longer had to limp, stumble, or falter, for the shackles had been removed completely. I was now released to begin walking straight and upright, free at last.

With holdalls and bags neatly lined up alongside the bus, ready for loading, and radiant hearts and souls enthusiastic to board, we said a fond farewell to our safe haven, selected a pew, and set forth to return to the Dallas/Fort Worth metroplex. I purposely chose to sit alone toward the back as I was pensive and needing time to reflect.

It is, of course, impossible to impart to someone else what had just happened to me, but a life was turned inside out and backward. I was not the person who boarded the bus five days earlier, and my life would never be the same. I had been freed, and I no longer felt the guilt and shame of the past. I was free to live as a daughter of Christ and a princess. This was a term I did have difficulty embodying, as the royalty in England was not exactly representative of the sentiments it was supposed to engender. Perhaps a Cinderella kind of princess could be accepted, but whatever way I chose to understand my position, I was special and unique in His eyes. And absolutely no one could rob me of that truth then, now, or in the future.

I was no longer in condemnation, and I was certainly not accountable to any single living person. I was to align myself under the one true light or be forever lost. I was seated in heavenly places in Christ, but what that meant in practice was an unknown and only later to be revealed in Jesus.

We all must make this choice one day, and it is one we can share thereafter. Each of us have been given the ability to exercise our wills, and we must each decide how to exercise them. What a privilege it is to be given the choice and not be forced into submission. God is a gentleman and respects each person's individual will. He waits.

Our journey back to Fort Worth was lengthy, and my mind was awash with new thoughts. Very clear instructions were given to me as to how I should move forward. I questioned these thoughts but somehow knew they were different. What I had been blessed to experience was to be shared with those outside the fold, those lying entrenched within the corporate world. I think my direction was being shaped. My real reason for being in the US was being unfolded, and my purpose was revealed, or so I thought.

Some seven hours later, we arrived with eyes glistening and faces that shone as though body glow had been applied. And much excitement filled the air as we stepped off the bus. A large group of past questers was eager to welcome us home, lining the road as the bus turned into the arrival church car park. Their joy was infectious. I, however, remained quiet as the magnitude of my salvation experience had overwhelmed me. I was almost cautious in my approach to people's questions, and I trod furtively through the inquisition.

I kept repeating, "I know that I know that I know."

Damascus Road, maybe not, but a turnaround so sharp that I was still spinning. Where next? What should I expect? I was vulnerable, naïve, and a newborn babe. That irritating comment that had been so fashionable in England of born again now had meaning as it had for my husband but a month earlier. I understood, but why had it taken me fifty-three years? Why so long?

Chapter 7

Why So Long?

Getting back to everyday living and life, the day Wednesday was almost surreal. I was back among familiar surroundings but felt a stranger in my own home. I felt coy and even a need to be shown around. On my return bus journey home, thoughts, words, and instructions had deluged my mind. You name it. I appeared to receive it. God's words were being downloaded into me. Did I know that?

At eight thirty on that Wednesday morning, what was a direct word to open the Bible at 1 Kings 2:2–3 and 1 Kings 3:5 in the Old Testament (yes, exactly) and write it down has continued to this day with over 350 handwritten pages of instructions, warnings, actual visions, titles of books and chapter headings, newspaper articles, poems, songs, and a whole myriad of topical discussion papers to be written, and with each and every one, supporting scriptures, chapters, and verses.

At that point in time, I didn't know my way around the Bible. Yes, I had read it sporadically, but knowing, quoting, and understanding it is surely a tall order. After all, I was raised a Catholic.

And here I was reading the Bible, 1 Kings. The day revealed verses from the Gospel of John and an Old Testament prophet, Jeremiah, a warning about a curse, an instruction to "write your heart out and right your heart out," two books with title and headings (with supporting scripture), four named discussion papers, a song, and a sermon entitled "How Long Is a Ministry?" Was I bemused or confused?

I was perhaps dazed, but what poured out onto paper was the Lord speaking through my pen. The speed at which it burst forth can only be explained in that way. I will share with you His first instruction:

"My heart is in your hands, Pamela. Your pen is my mouth; your emotions are my thoughts. I am all you need. Scriptures will be given, but let their attention not slip for a split second. They are lost then! Ground everything in my Word, and back it up for the unbelieving realm, but let it flow with no breaks. There is no opportunity or moment for deception. It breeds legions of doubt and centuries of joyless living. Act quickly. There is little time. Bring me my sheep quickly. The time is nigh. Be troubled not. It is time to open your eyes and see."

My pen name was to be Pamela Rose. "Why?" I asked.

He clearly replied, "You rose from the dead. You rose, you chose, and you obeyed and said, 'I am willing.' It is time."

I have since understood that the "fallen I" is the "risen we." Thank heavens!

So from my maiden name Pamela Sullivan to my matrimonial name of Pamela Polledri, I am now Pamela Rose. Three times around the block and then I got it! The day ended in the wee hours of the morning, and I was mentally drained. I laid an overly weary head down and slept soundly. The first time in years, I might add!

Over the next three days, the Creator Father reached down into my days with miraculous wonders. I can't explain them. Only they happened. Birds sang to me inside my interior dress closet of the bedroom. I was initially stunned, but I remembered how He had spoken to me at the ranch. This happened two days in a row. He was reminding me that He was very close at hand.

And at night as I went to bed, out on the balcony, heavenly chimes filled the air. I wondered if I was dreaming. It was melodic. The following day, I had to try to understand the sounds, so I scanned the property, but chimes could not be found. I admit that I even inquired if the next-door neighbor had any chimes. There were none. It seems like I was still a doubting Thomas.

I walked the full length of the balcony and looked over into our garden. As I did so, the sound of chimes echoed again at the other end. He was there! "Hear it now" is what I had been told, and I still questioned. Are we bizarre creatures or what?

Now it needs to be said that, at this point in time, I was unaware that the devil lurked and was waiting to get back inside the now newly cleaned house, me. He was eagerly attempting to plant seeds of doubt in my mind about the whole experience, and a bull's-eye across my heart had been placed. I was his target practice, but I didn't know that. He wanted me back in his pigpen.

I understood that I had now crossed over and was safe in the Father's hand and hidden in Christ in heavenly places, but I had not realized that the devil did not and does not release his possessions freely and will fight to the bitter end. Thank heavens for that Ephesian armor described in the Bible, although when you are still learning how to put it on to wear, time is needed before you can walk out in confidence. Satan's attacks were obvious, frequent, and reducing to subtle, but I had nothing to fear and everything to gain by standing firm.

I will relate one such attack because it was unpleasant in the extreme and involved a beautiful bird of prey. As I prepared to take my son to school early one morning shortly after my return from Quest, there on the lawn was a magnificent bird lying on its back with his head severed neatly. There were no feathers, no blood, and no head to be found. There were no signs of any struggle or killing, just a clean cut and placed right in full view for my benefit of course. Only the day before it had adorned our weeping willow tree in front of my home office window, and I had even remarked to friends about a wonderful bird that sat in the tree as if staring at me. This incident was there to unnerve and upset me, and it certainly achieved the latter. My obliging husband swiftly removed the bird, and I tried to blot out the picture from my mind.

Similarly, and this time with a little more malicious intent, he audibly and physically moved across our home with an act of hatred aimed to scare. It was midnight. I was writing the paragraph in this book that refers to our battle being against principalities and powers. I was alone in the house as my husband had gone to collect my son from a friend's home only minutes before. This took place the day after the bird fiasco.

As I was typing, an almighty noise suddenly broke out on the balcony outside our room, the one where the chimes had resonated. The balcony is sixty feet long and runs from one end of the house to the other. I was at my desk in the home office. I shot out of my chair, screamed, and became frantic. It sounded as though someone had picked up an iron bar and run it across the wooden posts of the balcony. There are eighty in total, so the mayhem was not a fleeting sound, but a well-purposed, loud, and frightening noise. As I began to flee from the room, I realized that was the evil one's intention, to stop me from writing and again to unnerve me. I realized he could not touch me physically. I was safe but shaken.

Happily my husband returned shortly thereafter. The following morning, we inspected the balcony and discovered five deep gouges had been left on one wooden post immediately outside the balcony door. To this day, we do not understand their significance and choose to ignore them.

Satan can be an annoyance, but I hear and see his approaches and miscellaneous guises. He can't harm me nor touch me again. Some of you will understand what I am saying, but for those of you wondering what on earth I am babbling about, I apologize. Like I said earlier, I get it. If you too will step out of the boat and walk on the water, yes, it may be a bit scary at first, but you'll get it too. Remember, you can't drown, and our Maker is there, waiting patiently. He just wants you to stop relying on yourself and your own reasoning and accept Him. It certainly does not make sense, but that is what faith is all about and what the word *trust* involves. He wants to hear you say, "Here I am, Lord. Please come into my life. I'm sorry."

So choose, friend, while you can, for the decision is yours alone. It's critical and absolutely essential!

Chapter 8

So What Next?

"Why so long?" I had uttered shortly after my arrival home.

Why so long indeed, and what next? In a nutshell, why did it take me so long to ask God into my life? Where did I think I was going all those years? Has this thought ever crossed your mind? I am sure it must have, but like every thought, it disappears into the mind's deep abyss. It gets caught up with all those other pressing, and not so pressing, thoughts. And somewhere in the wash, we must all get caught in the net.

Caught in the Net!

Where did my life go?
All those times, moments,
tests, and trials?
Things said, things done,
tears shed, mindless fun.
Laughter shared, ridicule dared.
Where did it all go?
Somewhere?
Nowhere?
Disappeared into oblivion?
For there is none!
Just gone?

How pointless is life
if that is all it was!

Empty breaths, striving,
gaining, and accumulating
into nothingness, born to die.
But what deception do I espy?
What stench lurks beneath the lie?
Where did my life go?
God swept up all trace,
leaving crumbs for man's embrace.

And back home He trawls us still
to cast His line, His daily nets to fill.
As fishers of men, He made you for me,
the expedition to join, no charge, it's free,
the burden of the catch, His, to hold.

Where did my life go?
Home!
Caught in the net!

For me, there could only be one answer. The cloak of deception was so great that the density of its weave had blinded me. What a march of pride had been on parade all my life, and I had not recognized one step taken. I had not been taught that my heart freely given was all that God wanted and nothing more. It never dawned on me that I had not in fact been born again. Like I said earlier, I had hated that phrase. It always sounded so crass. But for many years, a lifetime, I had lived religion and felt justified in so doing. Why? That is what I had been taught! But I was mistaken and badly deceived.

I suppose I just didn't get it. I went to church on occasion and did good (and not so good) deeds in my life. That was about the sum total of my commitment to God. I was locked into the squalor of indecision and blinded by religion, the sort that Jesus frequently warned against.

Happily, and from now and then on, I would not have to prove anything before God and know that He would be alive and active in my life. I merely had to stop trying to control and do the right things and instead be that person I was always intended to be, Pamela Rose.

He wanted to give me a key, a free gift, and all I had to do was take it. I had to surrender my heart and will to Him unconditionally. Once He had my heart, the light turned green, and the way ahead was clear. We could move forward. Prior to that, He was unable to work with me because my heart belonged to the world, my job, a business, and son. I was stuck on amber and going nowhere fast. Thank God that traffic lights have defined sequences and change! Green eventually comes.

An overt act of my own will exercised was the start. It had to be my choice first. No one could do that for me. No priest, no church, or no good works could assist. I had been drawn, and obedience was my unseen command. I had waved the white flag frantically, hoping it would be seen. And as it was spotted, it was lowered, and I was swept up in the palm of His hand, never to touch the ground again. "Safe in the Father's hands" makes admirable sense now.

Thank you. Thank you!

> And God will raise you up on eagles' wings,
> bear you on the breath of dawn,
> make you to shine like the sun,
> and hold you in the palm of His hands.

I comprehend these words now. I didn't prior to March 2, 2007, for they were just words devoid of any real meaning that accompanied a rather nice tune sung in church on Sundays. But now they made complete sense.

I have discovered that, when your heart belongs to Him and Him alone (not your husband, wife, child, mother, father, job, friend, and so on), you can confidently and safely get out of the boat, walk on the water, and live. You won't sink if you trust in Him alone. But if you choose to ignore the invitation, you can remain sitting awkwardly in the boat until it sinks, fully laden and overloaded with your life's worries, concerns, illnesses, anxiety, and treachery. And believe me, you will sink unless you surrender, take the lifeline extended, and get out quick.

Navigator

God is always coming toward us, never away!
He saw the storm, and He walked to them.
He climbed into the boat, to them.
And so into our hurricane He comes.
He speaks.
It stops!
He's in control.
Storms must obey Him.
Call Him on board,
to your storm, your hurricane.
You don't want to be a shipwreck, do you?

Be clearheaded, faithful, and true,
to Him who is able to do exceedingly and abundantly,
more than even faith can understand.
For only He is wise; only He knows you,
your storm.
To you be He, your captain.
Call Him, trust Him, and praise Him
always.
Navigator!

I had grabbed hold of my captain, my navigator, and I was being lifted and then lowered to higher ground, terra firma. It was a salvage operation, and it looked like this.

Rich Destitute

Destitute, now ready,
your condition ripe,
countenance settled.
Empty are you to receive
His power-filled life,
No pride to spoil or envy steal
the self now spent, sufficiency dead.
Rich destitute are you!
Prepared and ready to go,
make disciples of all nations.
Go!
Rich destitute of God are you,
Go!

Chapter 9

Terra Firma

As the days passed and I began to crawl along new terrain, my eyes began to adjust and see differently. My heart was beginning to beat in unison with His. I was able to see that my fellow man was blindly marching toward that precipice of indifference and complacency, into which he would spill. I had teetered on that very same edge for an age, mindless of its subliminal gravitational pull and all the while fixing my fate. But you know God knew me and my heart, and He was going to pursue me wherever and however many expeditions it would take.

I lived a lie for fifty-three years, but I get it now. I had been complacent. I had played the independent card, and I just hadn't taken enough time to consider life. I had been self-sufficient and almost smug, but when birds speak English to you, music plays where none can possibly play, birds sing to you in your clothes closet, and heavenly chimes sound across your home, you know there is change and supernatural power at work in your life.

I want to share one such incident with you because, in the natural world, it would have been impossible, yet it happened. And we all live, that is, my husband and son, to tell the tale. Imagine stepping out of a car that careered off the I-45 in Texas at seventy miles per hour, having done two full turns on the freeway during a Friday morning, ending up headlong in a ditch, without a scratch to the car or injury to the passengers or me, the driver!

Imagine. Someone else is in control, and He wants to get your attention and speak. He wants to awaken you from the empty busyness of life and sound the wake-up call loud and clear. He wants to let you know that He is there and close!

We had been returning home from a golf tournament in the Houston area of Texas with my son. It was a Friday morning, and there was plenty of traffic about and intermittent rain showers, some heavy. One minute, the car motored along in glorious sunshine, and the very next, torrential rain pelted against the windscreen as the wipers worked furiously to clear the screen. Without warning and in a split second, the car went completely out of control and quite literally glided across the freeway while the traffic behind came cascading down upon us.

In those anxious moments, as I attempted to handle an uncontrollable high-speeding vehicle, I recall saying to myself, "Oh no! We are going to end up in hospital today. Wait for the crash. We are going to be hit."

I waited as the car gracefully twirled around upon the freeway twice, and just as a dancing couple gracefully retires from the floor to waiting pews, we were meticulously placed (and I truly mean placed) into the roadside ditch at high speed.

How so? you must be thinking.

And I can quite understand any apprehension you may feel as to the authenticity of this story, but it happened. It is a story for your benefit and my heart. Quite simply, God was totally in control and just wanted me to know in a very big way. What's more, my son remained fast asleep in the back seat, blind to all that had gone on. I remember feeling mildly shaken but still inordinately calm.

Now the story does not end there! Within moments of settling into a rain-drenched, mud-filled ditch, a soft rap could be heard against the window. We all looked and saw a gentleman standing in the driving rain and inquiring as to our condition. He related to us that he had seen everything from behind and what he had witnessed was a miracle. He proceeded to walk the freeway to determine where we were so the police could be informed and a road recovery vehicle called. This he did, and he was not seen again.

And while this particular heaven-sent help was being conducted, more was to be orchestrated, all revealing God's magnificent hand. Two young men stopped to see if they could assist in pulling us out of the ditch. We erroneously believed this was the rescue service, but it was not. These were angels sent swiftly to our rescue to afford us the comfort we needed.

Within twenty minutes, the recovery truck arrived, and within a thirty-minute total, we were back on the rain-sodden freeway, continuing our journey home, with no damage and no burst or imbalanced wheels. We were put back onto the dance floor, heading home.

However, we did stop at the first gas station to clean some mud out of the tires, at the recommendation of the recovery crew. It was a surreal experience, one that could only have spelled disaster on a piece of paper, but I was learning that God does not deal with the seen only, but also the unseen, and this is where my faith was being built. And it was here that I was experiencing angels.

Now, where was I? Yes, imagine birds speaking. Grasp and fully digest that. Birds don't speak. They chirp! He wants each one of us to personally surrender hardened hearts and haughty intellect. In a nutshell, He wants us to come home freely while time is on offer. Soon it will dissipate and end. That is an irrefutable and absolute truth to which we all are subject.

You cannot prolong your life; neither can you reject its end. Psalm 90 reminds us that our days are numbered and the wilderness years of life are but a blink of an eye compared to our Maker's agelessness. He truly is all that He declares and more. He is the great I Am. Moses found that out.

I am a living witness to the good, the bad, and the ugly of life, and I survived. If you think death is the end, which it is not, but merely birth into a different realm, heaven or hell, isn't it worth hedging your bets now? God is there whether you believe it or not and always will be. You cannot change that fact. It is an objective truth, as is birth and death. Ignore it at your peril, and like fools heading for mass destruction, it will be too late when you take your last breath. If you don't accept the truth that there is one God, one physical death, one judgement, one heaven, and one hell eternal, then woe to you!

Let's put it another way. If you do not want to see hell's fury, then accept the free gift that He hands to you today unconditionally right now, that is, forgiveness and a future. Stop fighting yourself and surrender. He is and will be. Do not be concerned what others think about you, not even your family. Just step up to the mark and say, "I'm ready."

He is waiting for you. He so wants you to choose to trust Him, and He longs for that first look from you. He does not want you to make the wrong choice, and believe me, there is definitely a wrong choice to be made. I cannot fathom why we have such a problem believing this truth, other than that fear accompanies our belief system and we fervently believe we know it all and must be in control. We focus our attention on the past and what may happen in the future, the what-if type attitude rather than the present. We have only moments, not days or years. Just moments. So, we must learn to walk before we can ever run. Each new day taught me a fresh baby step, and even now I am but a toddler exploring and discovering new terrain. At least I now crawl on terra firma and no less.

Chapter 10

Change

As I said, "You have to learn to walk before you can run, but what a frustrating walk it can be. Falls, bumps, and bruises line the way, but none are too serious when He walks alongside."

At six thirty in the morning on Tuesday, March 13, 2007, just seven days after my return, God whispered for me to get up and said, "Let's write a while."

I asked sleepily, "Well, what am I going to write?" It's not a clever question, as I later found out.

"Listen," He said. "Draw from the well, for the future is bright. Draw from my love, and do what is right in my eyes, not yours. It is still hard to see, but I'm coming to visit with my heart's eternity. Go to a page and show them my heart, a plan to continue. And what is your part?

"It's big. It's bold. It's your long, passionate vision to help at the core. It's just a revision. You wanted a brand; I needed a heart. You wanted success; I needed your heart. Dear child, do listen and know it is true. It is I, God Almighty, who is writing in you and righting, I say, all that is wrong. Listen, my child. There's no time to prolong. The doors will open, and in you will step. There's no looking back. Great works lay ahead."

What was the purpose of these verses? Up to that point, I had followed my own self-sufficient life plan in the United Kingdom by trying to create the world's first legal brand. My limited reasoning said that, if Kellogg could do it for cereal and Coca-Cola for the drinks industry, why couldn't I do the same for legal services? Why not? We buy and live by brands. Why not make the law accessible in a way that the public understands? Help in some way. The problem was they were my plans and not His.

And for twelve long years, I did not discern this because I had my plan—my agenda—to follow. I didn't listen. I suppose I didn't know how to. The sooner we grasp the simple truth that we are not in control, the sooner we can begin to understand the depth of His mercy, width of His patience, and breadth of His love. It just cannot be measured or fathomed in our futile thinking.

Admittedly my heart was right about my company, and I was on the right track, per se, but my focus was misdirected, as was my purpose. I was looking in the wrong direction. I was chasing a brand that would, of course, die in time. I should have been chasing after truth and life, not short-term gains, fleeting success, and worldly accolades, but eternal truths. What a fool I had been, releasing twelve years of my life while chasing a dreamer's prize, only to discover an empty canvas hanging on my soul's wall. Mea culpa! Mea culpa!

So, let me again share with you the richness of words he spoke during those early, fragile weeks because they haunt me and cause a burden in my heart.

He said, "Pamela, provoke them to think, to wonder 'What is this light of life?' Without it, they are lost."

"They are lost" pierced deeply, and immediately an instruction to write "Love Lost Endures Forever" was born. Deep is the well of tears shed for this work, and it speaks like this:

Love Lost Endures Forever

Shipwrecked lives lay strewn 'neath earth's putrid layers,
and seas furies lay claim to unsuspecting souls.
The earth, but a graveyard of obstinacy
tightly packed, meticulously swallowed
and lost forever.

Loving hearts, hijacked by obsession,
and disfigured beyond recognition.
Hope cruelly robs subsiding smiles as destruction bellows
and deceit unveils its snare.
Caught!

What finery it adorns!
What palaces it frequents!
Free hearts savagely manipulated, massaged,
then battered and doomed to eternal darkness,
unbridled pain, and hopelessness.

Love's hand extended found rejection its glove.
Its enduring heart nailed for mercy's sake,
yet glory to behold in man's inhumanity
while curses wailed for sin's death eternal.

Majesty hung boldly to shame and claim
love's mutiny hijacked, lest carrion cry "Victory!"
Love is dead. See how it hangs! Lies!
Death's sentence delivered its blow.
It's over!
Resurrected!

Extend a battle-weary hand and defeat defiance.
Time's merciless march presses on and cries,
"Come, all who are weary and worn, let love's cloak
enfold you, life's promise capture you, and
new birth claim you. It is time.
For love lost endures forever!"

Be complacent, procrastinate, argue, and scoff whatever, but understand that "love lost endures forever" and there is no return once time expires. Love is our Creator.

So my changing days brought changing ways. I was being remodeled throughout. On Friday March 16, 2007, at 6:02 a.m., I was again awoken and hastened to write yet more verses and for women who hurt this time. I want to share these with you, perhaps to encourage but, most of all, to reassert that there is hope no matter how improbable it looks or how deeply it is buried. It can be uncovered and reached once surrender is complete. I give you the words as they were spoken to me, and for those of you who decide to follow the Quest as I did, your wilderness day may start out in this way.

"Please sit a while. Just listen. Be still.
I want your attention, your heart, and your will.
For there is no weather that can steal you away,
Divinely appointed, your presence today.
Please dry all of your tears
and release me your heart,
your life in my hands, I wish to impart.
Enough are your sorrows, your burdens, the pain.
Give me your torment, betrayal, your shame.
Embark on a journey into wilderness years,
there to lay to rest inequitable tears.
But let's travel quickly, there's so much to do.
My heart awaits eagerly that one word from you."

"Yes, dear Father, I surrender my retreat.
I cast down my life to lay at your feet.
I'm battered, I'm weary, I'm bruised, I feel worn.
I am ready to see now, to accept, to be born."

"If that is your wish, my dear lady, to be,
then step into my being and dare to be free."

He awaits that one word from you, "Yes."
To remain shackled throughout your life is not what is intended

and does not have to be sustained. Breaking free is 100 percent possible if you step out of that comfort zone, expose yourself, and hand over the driftwood of living, your life. It is not complicated, and it just requires one step of faith. You believe the sun is behind the clouds, even if it can't be seen, so what is the problem believing there is life after this earthly one and a life to be lived to the full? Why hesitate or doubt? What holds you back? Reason? Logic? Rationale? Intellect? Fear? What can you conceivably know that the Creator hasn't already made available to discover? We are fallible and but a breath away from earthly death. Perhaps the following poem will speak to your heart and help you see more clearly.

You Leave It All! Psalm 49 Speaks!

So many an hour you broke your back
to find a way to feed your clan.
So many a moment, lost in time,
you surrendered the precious
to gain the wind! And then?
Puff! It disappeared!
Your time, your life, but vapor
daily dissipating into unseen realms.

Did you see it go, silently leaving you behind
to tread the pavements of discontent
in search of all that matters not?
Did you swallow the lie?
One-time round is all you have!
Despicable deceit, dressed to kill,
one more victim into the hole seduced.
Or did you look above, ahead and see?

He promises to be the inheritance
no eye has seen nor ear has heard,

not left behind, but forward sewn.
He bids you plant while time is known,
to toil to leave behind what's dead
when brilliant life ahead instead
awaits your will in surrender He'll say,

"Welcome, repentant tears. This is the day!"
Pamela Rose
Palm Springs to Dallas midair, December 22, 2013

I firmly believe we all have understanding of Him, but like mules, we remain obstinate and resolute that we want to go our way, and of course, we know better!

Can you begin to see the web of deceit that the devil spins? He is a master at his craft, and the tapestry he displays is exciting, enticing, and inviting, but its threads are all meticulously laced with deadly poison, ready for the kill. I apologize if I offend any readers, for no offense is intended, but I cannot sit back any longer and watch my fellow man walk headlong into a fiery furnace. I am not an innocent bystander. I am a witness to a truth that I can no longer deny or disown.

God exists, and His Son Jesus Christ came to this earth to save us from our sin and to give us a gift of love called eternal life. Put more crudely, it is to save us from the biblical hell. (And that's everlasting too!) Look what Jesus went through for an obstinate and thankless race. Understanding what took place at the crucifixion of the man Jesus Christ is a mystery, I concur, but one we can embrace should we care to.

To this day, I too struggle with this mystery, but I must continue to walk regardless of my thinking mind. The self is somewhat reminiscent of baking brownies. Have you ever had to wash the bowl afterward? Lots of sticky mixture is caked to the sides. You have emptied the bulk of the mixture, but there is still residual mix.

That's a bit like sin. The residue is cleansed as we walk our walk of faith, just as we wash that brownie mixture bowl. Full-scale strikes will be launched to divert the washing up, but to no avail. Sin has no hold on any person who has surrendered his life to God through Jesus Christ. Some mixture will be more difficult to remove because it has set, but it will be removed in time. I trust you have embraced the double entendre and understand that sin can no longer bind or condemn you. It has lost its sting or grip, as has death. Hallelujah!

But please note that sin's power is only removed if and when you accept Jesus Christ into your life and acknowledge Him as the Savior and source of life eternal. There is absolutely no other way, however you may squirm and deliberate. None! The bowl has to be cleaned!

Chapter 11

Chayil!

As the days galloped on ahead from my release, I have daily learned the intricacies of *chayil*, the Hebrew word for "freedom" and one to which I had acquiesced.

"How?" you may ask.

Let me tell you how freeing freedom actually is in the fallen world in which we find ourselves. His miracles did not stop, and He poured them upon me fast and furiously.

You will recall that my life had been a colorful display of futile thinking, glamorously clad in so-called high living and my penchant for alcohol, damaging in the extreme. To all intents and purposes, I had a lifelong addiction or, should I say, "fatal attraction" to alcohol to varying degrees from the age of twenty all the way up to fifty-two.

Imagine! So where was it now? In a word, it was gone! In a split second, God removed from me not only the desire to enjoy a drink and need a drink, but He had completely rearranged my thinking. He allowed me to experience the freedom to attend a party and not even want or think about having a drink. What's more, I could enjoy myself without getting inebriated. For so many years, I had secretly dreaded attending yet another "do" because I knew that controlling my drinking addiction was nigh impossible. But now I had been freed, and the suggestion that willpower was responsible for the outcome was total nonsense.

I say this merely because a family member could not accept my deliverance and attributed it only to my exercise of willpower.

Nothing could be further from the truth. God saw my total surrender, and He took away the floating debris. God saw my belief and passion and gave me further relief and miraculous signs. After all, I was born again. The washing up had begun in earnest.

Another such miraculous sign in the form of a healing was the total release from my parade of allergies. Since the age of eleven, you may recall that I had been allergic to animals. These increased in diversity through the years to include hayfever, perfume, mold, and newspaper, to name but a few. I suspect for some of you reading that you can empathize with me and know just what I am talking about. I had suffered from pesky allergies requiring umpteen tests to determine identity, and then duly prescribed medicine to alleviate the ensuing discomfort. This had been my lifetime thorn.

Today as I write, it's a memory but also a source of encouragement for others still captive to the allergy vice. The euphoria at being able to pick up a cat or mind the neighbor's dog has been very real. To enjoy my son's golf tournaments without weeping and irritable eyes that I used to want to scratch out of their sockets has absolutely been a Godsend. And the icing on the cake has been the joy of being able to spray myself with perfume. Oh, sweet scent, how pleasurable thou art!

It sounds trifling in its sentiment, but unreservedly I declare the healing to be grand beyond expectation. I had always lived with allergies, and they had become a way of life, part of the weave, but not so anymore. Forgiven and freed. *Chayil* and hallelujah!

My days revealed to me how my focus was shifting from I to Him, that is, from mine to His. I was learning to walk alone in the seen and with a full entourage accompanying me in the unseen realm. What traffic jams must exist in these realms when a saved person is starting to walk. What battalions must escort that creative beauty as either he or she begins to toddle upright and free. Daily I became aware of my absolute need to remain firmly in touch with my new friend, Father, and confidante because I knew that mortal man was nothing without Him. We cannot exist independently of

Him for He is our lifeblood. Only He is able to reconcile our lives, our differences, our inequities and our souls.

Reconciliation for All, If ...

If light shines,
where does darkness live?
If you know,
where does understanding start?

If right points to wrong,
where does morality determine?
If the earth exists,
where does creation reside?
If science questions,
where does reason explain?

Can a heart beat alone or
a body function without?
Can a brain operate apart or
emotions penetrate matter?

If we acquiesce to evil,
how can we reconcile the conscience?
If we breathe we live and
if man is,
how can I Am not be?

For our will dictates choice of eternity,
but if there is none, breathe no further.
Futility reigns!
Not so!

We are inseparable in our being.

> Our essence is defined,
> and we quite simply are because He is.
> And because He is, we can be
> His!
>
> Pamela Rose
> January 4, 2008, Southlake, Texas

It matters not what beliefs you hold, for at the end of your appointed days, you will meet your Maker, whether you like it or not. You cannot change the outcome on earth, but has it dawned on you that you can change your future thereafter?

For many, you will say, "Sorry, once you're dead, you're dead, so live, eat, drink, and be merry. Do as you please. It's all about number one!"

But I want to share sobriety with you! And what do I mean? Let me please give you chilling words that were given to me on March 16, 2007. "You do not have the luxury of death."

Embrace that statement well and meditate before you move on. Fully consider the consequences of rejecting God. Deliberate the consequences of lukewarm, mediocre faith, the "as and when it suits" type of faith. "You do not have the luxury of death!" That hurts and quite frankly terrifies me. I will, if I may, illustrate the point with a chilling true story, abbreviated to respect every reader's personal beliefs and opinions.

A lady in a hospice was being monitored, and medical readings suggested she was close to death. Family had been called. In the interim, a man of the cloth came to ask her if she knew Jesus Christ. The response was a fading no and a determined unwillingness to accept this name. He pressed the point and begged her to repeat a few small words of salvation. She remained firm and even found words to deny the existence of Jesus Christ. Monitors began to sound, and she, in her dying moment and last breath, exclaimed, "Oh no! I am going into flames. Oh, the flames! I am burning." With a final gasp, she expired!

For now, I shall not elaborate further, but I believe she was experiencing something that is repeatedly spoken about in the Bible. You see, she did not have the luxury of death. Yes, she died physically, but that was not the end, and she had made her choice. I shall leave you to determine what she was experiencing as she was being sucked into earthly death. A grim reaper indeed awaits.

The poem that follows further considers the choice. Take some time and absorb that there is no exit and no way out. It may fuel the imagination just enough to reconsider death.

No Way Out!

All there is to provide, God provides.
All there is to say, God has spoken.
All there is to see, eyes were created.
All there is to hear, ears fashioned.
All there is to live for, He commanded.
All that life comprises, Jesus has fulfilled.
All the end can bring, God has designed.
It is written.
It is finished.
There is but one ending for us all, death.
There is no way out.

Death will usher in a new dimension,
life into eternal darkness or into eternal light.
Which will you this day accept?

Receive while time exists,
for there is an end, that day.
It is written.
Believe or disbelieve.
It cannot change finality,
the end.

It is written!

O' death, friendless cheat,
there is no way out!
There is no peace in death,
if darkness is your light today!
Let light be your darkness today.
God in you forever then.
It is written.
No way out!

Friend, don't be proud. Don't go that route. There is another road. Take it. God has given us all a blueprint for living embodied in the books of the Bible and made alive in the life of the person, Jesus Christ. He lived and breathed, and He died. He was the embodiment of God Himself. Jesus did rise from the dead, and not a soul on this planet can disprove otherwise. The crucifixion was witnessed, as was the empty tomb and His resurrected body. This is not fiction, something to decide whether you want to believe or not. It is an objective truth that will exist whatever you choose to think. Hollywood's movie *Risen* even grappled with this truth. No physical body could be found! The tomb was empty! Death did not hold him! We don't have that luxury, just a new beginning!

To survive on this planet, we do have a guidebook and a map, effectively the Bible, which we have to follow at all times if we want to reach the destination! Should you get a little lost on your way, don't worry. He has many scouts that He sends out to get you back onto His narrow road home.

Now, if you determine that you are not going to use it and prefer to go your own way, then you do know what you have to look forward to. Our lady in the illustration has graphically warned us, and as helpless and desperate as she must have felt, it was too late. She was alone and without God's protection.

In her cry "Oh, the flames," you will be left in a world without light, love, or hope. You will be lost forever, and hell's suite will be your eternity. Is that really what you want? Dear reader, I don't wish to sound harsh, but I have been told to write boldly and to shake up complacency in the hearts of man. I am to stir the imagination and our selfish streak and to vividly paint the picture of eternity without God. It is grim and terrifying to be precise, and it is real!

Warnings are given throughout the Bible and are unmistakable in their intention and frequency. Swallow pride, rational thinking, human wisdom, and scientific reasoning and step up to the mark. Talk to the air—because that is what it will seem like to you in your rational thought process—and say, "I'm sorry for my behavior and for things I have done and said. I'm sorry that I have hurt so many people. I want to know you. I want to have you in my life. I want to follow your map. I want to be new and redressed. I want to have eternity, and I will surrender my heart and rights to you alone. I acknowledge you are my Maker, my Father, friend, healer, and shelter. No one can replace you. I repent and confess all that I know to be wrong and all that I am unaware is wrong. Please show me the way forward. Thank you."

Many of you reading right now will say, "What absurd nonsense and arrogant assumptions she makes!"

But I stand firm, having been removed from a pit and proclaim that God is real. I met Him. I experienced His power repeatedly. I saw evil, and it fought ferociously to pull me back. There was a battle for my soul, and God's will prevailed. Why? I had made the conscious decision and choice to surrender to Him once and for all and not a little bit here and a little there or sometime later. My all was required, and that comprised my whole heart.

You see, He already knew the condition of my heart when I arrived on March 2, 2007, and He knew my motives were right. I was finished with the lie, and I was going to find life. But also remember and accept without protest that the surrender of your life to God will not automatically open the way to worldly success and financial stability. He knows your heart and your motives, so beware! He knows your why, the reason you do something, just as He knows His because of His will.

May I urge you right now, if you are feeling anxious, uncertain, doubtful, angry, condescension, superior, enraged, inquisitive, or hurt, to accept that this is God's prompting in your heart. What you are experiencing is His invitation to you to enter through the gate and into His peace. Remember, the gate is narrow, as is the road that leads to heaven. And so too is the gate wide and the road broad that leads to destruction, and you have to make a choice between the two.

He invites you to step out of your comfort or discomfort zone and walk toward Him. Do you want to get well? That is a loaded question, requiring a cautious yet carefully considered response. He will sustain you, though you may stumble many times, and that is a promise! Not a man-made empty promise, but one that is richly true. He will equip you with all you need to make it on the journey home inside an old body, but with a new you embodied! You must be fully prepared to get up and walk whatever the route back, and He is always at your side accompanied by hosts of angels. (Alas, the subject of another book!)

So, it is your choice and yours alone. Your will, a most gracious and wonderful gift that is greatly misunderstood and misapplied, invites you to meet Him when you choose to do so. Do it now. Don't procrastinate any longer, for time is not your possession. It is but a reprieve in which you decide your eternity. You have to choose or lose life. I spent fifty-two years of my life searching for that elusive next fix, thrill, buzz, achievement, or what. We all have that longing because God sowed eternity into our hearts, no matter where we are on this planet. The problem seems to be that we just don't understand what that longing is that we all share. It's there within each one of us and is that *je ne sais quoi* of daily living, that indeterminate desire for something tangible to make sense of life as we live it. It is that hope that we were born into and hope that must be seized and accepted so as to birth freedom into our lives with the unshackled ability to start our journey back home.

John Bunyan's much acclaimed work *The Pilgrim's Progress* scrupulously maps out the journey with a perception so deep that it begs the question, "Did God reveal Himself to John in his prison cell to enable him to be a solid witness to life's journey?"

No one knows, but his wisdom and understanding remains profound. If you have not read the book, please take the time to do so. It will change you, but for some, you may still be saying …

I've Lost My Way

I've lost my way; I can't see.
Where am I?
I'm disconnected,
no longer turned on.
How do I get back?
But get back where?
I've lost my way!

I've lost my way; I can't hear
my heart beating.
There is only silence
pounding in my ear.
Droplets of sweat
are witnessing.
I've lost my way!

I've lost my way; I cannot think.
Who I am now?
Bedlam strangles
my aching mind
as I walk empty thoughts
down lonely streets.
I've lost my way!

Please find me; bring me home.
I've lost my way!

Chapter 12

Let's Begin Again

As we arrive at the end of this book, you may observe that it continues. It doesn't really end, for only fiction has that luxury! No, all we do is continue into the next chapter of our particular story and unique to us. This thought brings to mind a scripture found in the gospel of Luke 8:8 which reads - "*He who has ears to hear, let him hear.*" When Jesus cried these words, He alone knew the heart, soul and mind of man, and He alone knows who will 'hear' this book. His most urgent appeal wrote the poem that follows and it may even help you to 'hear'.

A Blank Page

A blank page, and New Year ahead
stand ready to unfold its secrets
and bury tyrant memories
that seek to taunt, haunt, and undo!
Yet not so!
I smell a lie wafting near!
The past is passed. Morte!
All consequences but dying embers
left un-stoked, for still hope awaits
faithfully, your willing heart to enter,
your page to fill.

Will you see His hand,
hear His call alighting upon
now-deafened ears, blind indifference,
yet still urging, prompting your attention?
Yes, another moment to seize hope's hand,
a New Year or plummet anew headlong into
the dark's lure, unaccompanied.
Fair game are you!

What will it be friend of mine unknown
hope or reason's draw?
Faith, fear, or folly?
Still a blank page!
Fill it wisely.
Fill it now with hope's pen,
Jesus Christ.

"I know that I know that I know," and I am eternally bound in His plan of love and salvation for mankind, loved with a love that I do not fully comprehend. You did not evolve on the back of a crystal or appear for no other reason than to just breathe. You have been created in His likeness, redeemed, and reconciled to the Creator. You see, there is something to be saved from, and it is inescapable if you, of your own self-will, choose to disbelieve that God does exist. I do not wish to labor the point nor cause anxiety in your hearts, but I do want to rock complacency. I do want to make you think.

So, what can I say in closing that I have not already said? Be earnest and repent because He stands at the door of your heart and knocks. If you hear his voice (if you feel doubt or uncomfortable), open the door, and He will come into your life in a split second. Just let Him in. I did.

The Voice

Not the voice of convenience do I hear.
Nor the clamor of confusion,
teeming around,
jostling,
cajoling,
vying for a place in my ear or
my heart to overload and burden.
No, not that voice do I hear!

No, I hear the voice of freedom crying out,
"It is finished" to those with ears to hear
forlornly squatting amidst blood-filled pools
while darkness settles, skies thunder, and
truth hangs in His will for all to see!

That voice speaks through the ages,
gently, persistently, and reassuringly whispering,

"I am here; I am near, never far, with you
on your way home, longing to hear
that sweet sound of desire murmuring."

"Abba Father, I'm coming back now.
I hear You, Your voice
in love compelling me
to follow You and return.
Yes, I hear you!"

Stop fighting. It is of no use. His Will will prevail, no matter how much you scoff, rant and rave, belittle, or reject.

Something niggles you, doesn't it? It gnaws away daily, demanding attention. It is time to know that you know that you can know. Discard pride and lofty thinking, and open that door. Time is on the timer, and it is running out. He gives us time enough and then no more. Stand and be counted, and respond today. Hear it now. Hear it now. Hear it now. And into the fray you can march forth, victorious and free.

Into the Fray!

The end of possibility reached.
Empty and free I stood.
All that was no longer is
my funeral attended.
I am ready!

"Rise up, children of God. Rise up!
The door is open, and the battle at hand.
Don't fear, stand firm and free
in His Almighty power,
covered by His love
and His increasing glory!

Stand! Stand and be counted now!
The Faithful One has sounded the call.
Respond today! Your funeral has passed.
And ready are you to stand.
Be armed, equipped, established, and sent
into the fray,
that magnificent, mysterious delay!

Yes, into the fray, you must go!"

Epilogue

When opinion has found its forum
and the silent verdict delivered,
the measure of a book is but the
weight of the heart left behind!

                                        Pamela Rose

Printed in the United States
By Bookmasters